BEHIND THE GREEN CURTAIN

D0064099

3 1705 00190 5964

BEHIND THE GREEN CURTAIN

The Sacrifice of Ethics and Academics in Michigan State Football's Rise to National Prominence

STU WHITNEY
AND
BOB KOURTAKIS

STATE LIBRARY OF OHIO
SEO Regional Library
Caldwell, Ohio 43724

MASTERS PRESS

Published by Masters Press, 5025 28th Street, S.E., Grand Rapids, MI 49512

© Copyright Stu Whitney and Bob Kourtakis, 1990

All rights reserved

No part of this publication may be reproduced, stored in a retrieval system, or transmitted, in any form or by any means, electronic, mechanical, photocopying, recording, or otherwise, without the prior written permission of Masters Press.

Printed in the United States of America
First edition

Credits
  Cover design: Tracey L. Gebbia
  Front cover photo: David Olds
  Back cover:
    Headlines reprinted with the permission of the Detroit *News*,
      a Gannett newspaper, © 1990
    Headline reprinted with the permission of the Lansing *State*
      Journal, © 1990

Library of Congress Cataloging-in-Publication Data

Whitney, Stu, 1967–

  Behind the green curtain: the sacrifice of ethics and academics in Michigan State football's rise to national prominence / Stu Whitney and Bob Kourtakis. — 1st ed.

          p.   cm.

    ISBN 0-940279-33-9

  1. Michigan State University—Football—History. 2. College sports—Michigan—Moral and ethical aspects. 3. Athletes—Education—Michigan. I. Kourtakis, Bob, 1966–   . II. Title.

GV958.M5W47   1990   90–43860
                                                                      CIP

DEDICATION

To the guys at Virginia, who kept me interested, and to my mother, who kept me honest.

– Stu Whitney

To my brother Tony and young athletes everywhere. May the games still hold magic for you—even after adults mess everything up.

– Bob Kourtakis

CONTENTS

ACKNOWLEDGMENTS

It is impossible to complete a project as extensive as this alone. You need help, insight, and information from others to create a well-rounded picture.

So, in that spirit, we would like to thank the following people who took the time to be interviewed for this project: George Byam, Jeff Case, Travis Davis, William Donahue, Sam Eliowitz, Todd Elsea, Blake Ezor, Jenny Grau, Otis Gray, Lynn Henning, Cherryl Jensen, Craig Johnson, Mark Kaczmarek, David Kiel, David Kragt, Rory Leidelmeyer, Peter Levine, Tony Mandarich, Bobby McAllister, Steve McCornack, Tim Moore, Nagesh, Scott Parente, Dean Pridgeon, Kim Rahar, Bill Rankin, Brad Reaume, Derrick Reed, Harry Reed, Bob Reynolds, Beth Shapiro, Pat Shurmur, Elizabeth Smith, Mike Staisil, Mark Tabbacini, Eileen Van Tassell, Harry Wright, John Wright, and Dave Yarema.

Several research documents were also consulted in compiling information for this book. They include: *Chronicle of Higher Education,* February 22, 1989 and July 5, 1989; *Hormonal Manipulation: A New Era of Monstrous Athletics,* by Dr. William Taylor; "Intercollegiate Athletics and Big-Time Sport at MSU," by Beth Shapiro; *Journal of the American Medical Association,* January 23, 1987 and October 8, 1989; MSU football media guides; MSU graduation term books, MSU registrar's office records, and MSU salaries index; past taped interviews with George Perles and others; *Sports Illustrated,* January 5, 1987; *The Physician and Sportsmedicine,*

February 1990; and *U.S. News and World Report,* September 15, 1986.

Of course, thanks are also in order for the more than 100 players, coaches, and administrators who have contributed to our coverage of Michigan State football over the past four years. The openness and availability of those within the Spartan program, unlike those at many other schools, allowed this project to be possible.

And a special salute to three people. Without their efforts and support, this project would never have left the ground: Tom Bast, who supplied a forum to discuss these issues; Masters Press editor Amy Wolterstorff, for her patience and expertise; and Kimberly Gaudin, whose suggestions and detail work were essential to completing this text.

INTRODUCTION

*"I don't want to make a million dollars.
Hell, I just want to play football."*

    – former Spartan Tim Moore

We never really wanted to know about the ethical sacrifices involved in creating a national football power.

We never wanted to know how a football coach could let a star player spend finals week in jail—causing him to fail his classes—in order to have him ready to compete, or how student-athletes could be coaxed into unchallenging areas of study just to stay eligible. We never wanted to know that young men would flood their systems with illegal muscle-enhancing drugs in an attempt to make themselves as big and as strong as coaches thought they should be. Or that athletes often are lured into attending a school based on the dream of reaching the professional game—although the vast majority of these youngsters fall tragically short of this goal. Or how the power of a football program can mysteriously erase the unlawful deeds of its members.

We never wanted to know how wrong the whole thing really was.

It is impossible to spend any length of time around a major college football program without being disturbed by some of the trends that exist. Slowly, our romantic visions of the American football dream began to crumble. They gave way to some cynical questions and some rather disturbing answers. When we decided in October 1989 that these tendencies might be less dangerous if brought to light, we lacked the qualifications to investigate the issues on a national scale. What we knew was Michigan State University football. But we didn't know it as well as we thought.

Perhaps by offering this microcosm of the institution of college football, we can have some small influence on reforms which are sorely needed to make this business the game it once was.

Our critics will likely ask why the side effects of a program's success should warrant so much attention. Indeed, we are reminded of an after-hours journalism lecture by Iowa Coach Hayden Fry during the 1988 Big Ten summer meetings in Chicago. "I don't understand why there is so much negativism in the press these days," he said. "Why can't you guys concentrate on all the good things that happen?" Yes, there are some good things, but too many bad things are happening for us to look away any longer. College football isn't just Saturday afternoons in the sun; it is also the educating and nurturing of young men's talents and virtues. That is why exposing and understanding this moral corruption is so important.

We are not alone in this call to reform. The condition of collegiate athletics today is appalling, and the evidence is everywhere. Half of the NCAA's Division 1-A schools were censured, sanctioned, or put on probation in the 1980s. A 1989 sports ethics conference at the University of Rhode Island concluded that the burden placed on programs to generate a winner places too much pressure on coaches and sports officials, who often turn to cheating or unethical behavior. "The letter of NCAA rules isn't violated as much as you might think, but the intent is hammered to hell," Duke Head Basketball Coach Mike Krzyzewski said at the meeting. "The attitude is, 'How can I make these rules work for my situation?'"

Too often, this bending of morals comes at the expense of unsuspecting athletes. "We have a national scandal on our hands," said Northeastern University's director for the Study of Sports and Society, Richard Lapchick, in *U.S. News and World Report.* "For schools to admit students who are below their standards puts the youngsters at a tremendous disadvantage. To put them into the highly pressurized sports world compounds the sin."

Though the problems are greater than ever before, they have existed since the game's inception. Consider the following insight from Shailer Matthews, a dean at Chicago Divinity School during the late 1800s: "Football today is a social obsession. Football today is a boy-killing, education-prostituting, gladiatorial sport. It teaches virility and courage, but so does war."

It was with these concerns in mind that we decided to look a little more closely at the Michigan State University football program. Of course, there may be those who think we were biased against the program from the beginning and that this is an effort to create scandal where none exists. Our only defense against this charge is to say that this project is meant to be neither malicious nor monumental. However they appear, the issues presented here are meant to stimulate thought and to air certain problems so they can be publicly debated. Our goal is not to point at specific infractions, but to expose unhealthy attitudes and philosophies that contradict the traditional purpose of a university.

Yes, Lorenzo White's roommate says the superstar received plane tickets to Florida, courtesy of Michigan State University. Yes, Andre Rison was given free athletic apparel by agent Charles Tucker while still an amateur, according to an Okemos store owner. Yes, these are both National Collegiate Athletic Association violations. But there is a deeper and ultimately more meaningful reality here: The utopian values flaunted by MSU Coach George Perles are superseded and compromised by a voracious and insatiable appetite for success.

"To suggest it is some paragon of virtue, or that football builds character and wonderful men who graduate and go on to wonderful careers, is a total sham. The proof is in his [Perles] protesting too much about what a beautiful program it is," says Peter Levine, noted author and sports history professor at Michigan State University.

Maybe George Perles believes he has built a program that is a paragon of virtue, and maybe not. Perhaps most, if not all, coaches at some point compromise their sense of right and wrong to win ball games and keep their jobs. After all, they're no different from the rest of us, and who, at one time or another, has not sacrificed principle for expediency? George Perles' tragic flaw is his refusal to concede that point.

"Some of the values that he puts out to the public are ridiculous, but I think he believes what he's saying," says Sam Eliowitz, who played football with Perles at Detroit Western High School. "Whether they're true or not, he believes them. And that's all that matters to him."

George Perles sets such lofty goals for himself and his program that the failure to follow through on his promises is inevitable. It results in an angry backlash of resentment from a disappointed public and media. That's why he often greets controversy with a puzzled look, as if to say, "Why me?" He plays the role of the victim and, in a small way, he is.

"He doesn't say everyone is the way he would like them, but he does say he's going to try to get them there," says MSU assistant coach Pat Shurmur. "He never said that everyone was as smart as Dean Altobelli, or as talented as Percy Snow, or has the family life I do, but he does say that's what he's shooting for. He's not God, he's not a miracle worker. But they ask him to be."

It is the responsibility, then, of a coach to ignore those expectations and follow a path he himself considers just. George Perles has not done that. There have been too many instances of deceit, too many inconsistencies surrounding the academic integrity of his program, to believe him any longer. So we begin an inside look at four years of the Perles era—four years when MSU football went from pretender to power—in an attempt to find specific instances of compromised values and to discover why these have happened.

If those who read this book find the information half as enlightening as we did distressing, then we will consider the project worthwhile.

1

GEORGE PERLES

"You couldn't have a good time if it were Christmas."

> – George Perles to a reporter,
> November 25, 1989

There was something unmistakably different about George Perles when he sauntered into Michigan State's Crossroads Cafeteria on January 28, 1988. A short man, he walked tall, and people watched with the quietly respectful interest of a child eyeing a parent. Here was a hero, after all. Here was a true Spartan who, fresh from a professional football odyssey, had returned home in 1983 to more fanfare and relief than Odysseus enjoyed. "Let George do it!" screamed the masses. "Give me five years!" was his reply. And George did do it. After the fifth season, 1987, Michigan State won its first Rose Bowl since 1956 and it was sweet triumph, sweet reward. For people who had seen and heard enough of the maize and blue mystique, it was suddenly easy being green if you were from East Lansing. If you were from Ann Arbor, you were green with envy.

3

Perles, on this clear and windy Thursday afternoon, told his followers how he had raised his mighty sword and slain another beast for his homeland. He told how he had turned away the Green Bay Packers.

"When I had the opportunity, I could not leave Michigan State," Perles said from behind a small desk as about 150 media people and well-wishers looked on. "You could say I had a weakness and didn't go, or that I had a strength and didn't go. But what you can underline is that it's a fact I didn't go."

The media people did underline it. Athletic Director Doug Weaver, standing nearby, smiled with a strange sort of pride. And Perles, hair carefully combed, tie perfectly straight, stared directly ahead with a look not of finality, but of a curious new beginning.

Perles had heard from the Packers on Monday, January 25 and learned that he had the head coaching job with them if he wanted it. He then left on a recruiting trip and Tuesday night met formally with Packers officials in Chicago from eight until around midnight. Both Packers President Robert Parins and Vice President of Football Operations Thomas Braatz were present, and the final terms of the contract offer—five years, $2.25 million —were presented. Perles then returned to his Okemos, Michigan home where at 11:30 the next morning he met privately with Weaver, his close friend and boss, for almost four hours.

They were joined by their wives and, eventually, by Michigan State insiders. Former Spartan player and coach Hank Bullough, who was to become Green Bay's defensive coordinator, was present. (Two years later Bullough was named as a possible successor to Perles in the event that the New York Jets proved more successful than the Packers in wooing Perles from MSU.) Provost David Scott and Vice President for Finance and Operations Roger Wilkinson, two extremely powerful men in the

Michigan State chain of command, stopped by to show their support. Perles also spoke on the phone to Michigan Governor James Blanchard, a close friend and MSU grad, and to former MSU President John Hannah.

It was quite a surprise party, this gathering of indecision and politics and clandestine promises. And, while the music played (the same old song), reporters camped out at the Duffy Daugherty Football Building on campus waiting for news. Any news.

"I don't know where he is," Sports Information Director Ken Hoffman repeatedly told a handful of reporters—who knew he was lying but also knew he was told to lie, making it more pitiful than malicious. Reporters who ventured to the Perles home were met by his wife, Sally, who eventually said an announcement would be made the next morning. She then gingerly closed the door on the affair for the night, and reporters rushed home to speculate for the general public.

"I've never hidden from anybody," Perles said the next day, after announcing that morning his intention to stay. "Yesterday evening, I needed to be involved in this very seriously, and I didn't want any distractions. There was never anything said that wasn't true."

But the whole premise of this football feel-good festival, Perles' resolution to resist temptation, was not completely honest. The coach's five-year rollover contract was now a concrete ten-year deal, quite obviously an incentive to keep Perles from leaving. Perles had not seen men with power, men with money, fight over him since MSU bought him from the USFL's Philadelphia Stars. It was an exciting concept, to be sure, but it was even more: It was something to build on, something to use. Perles is fond of flipping through his speaking engagements during private chats with reporters, perhaps because it makes him feel both secure and superior to reinforce the idea that people would pay money to hear him talk.

The appeal of this man had always been his blue-collar mentality, his respect for the manly traits only the streets of Detroit could produce. But that had changed by the time he got up to leave Crossroads Cafeteria on that Thursday afternoon in January. Perles had won the Rose Bowl, and now he was seeing how much idolatry, how much respect, and how much money a winning football coach could expect in a sports-crazed society. "The only guy who gets no knocks for the winter is the guy who wins the championship," Perles said a year later. "When we won the Rose Bowl, there were no knocks at all. Everybody was nice. Everything was beautiful!"

So, when he finished extolling his undying love for MSU and everybody within, a crowd of relieved people approached him for reasons that were not completely clear. Some didn't even speak; they could not think of words for what they were feeling. Some just touched his shoulder, others stood by the desk and thought how lucky they were to be so near such a man. And Perles? Well, Perles sat there smiling, sporting the look of a man who had just discovered the most glorious thing in the world.

◆ ◆ ◆

On that day George Perles became more than a football coach; he became a football icon. The emotional outpouring of Spartan affection transcended mere wins and losses. Suddenly, Perles was national news. There was something noble and inspiring in turning down a multimillion-dollar contract to be true to your school. He became a symbol.

But is the loyalty to MSU that Perles so readily accepted as a symbol of his integrity a consistent value? Or is it one of several major contradictions in his carefully molded personality that have become apparent since he was lured back to MSU in 1983?

"I have tremendous loyalty to MSU and simply can't leave," Perles said after shunning the Packers, who eventually hired Cleveland assistant Lindy Infante. "I'm afraid you're stuck with me forever." But by "forever" he apparently didn't mean, well, forever. Two years later, after a 1989 Aloha Bowl victory over Hawaii, New York Jets General Manager Dick Steinberg met with Perles on New Year's Eve in Los Angeles to discuss bringing MSU's hero to the Big Apple. And those same old temptations came to the fore.

They were temptations that waged war with the genuine feelings Perles has had for MSU since he arrived as an All-State offensive guard in 1956, or maybe even before he arrived. "He sure wanted to go there," says Bill Rankin, a freshman quarterback at Detroit Western High School at the time Perles was a senior there. "He considered it a great honor." Despite suffering a career-ending knee injury during his sophomore year, Perles has often said his college days in East Lansing were the fondest memories of his life. It was there he met and married his wife, Sally Bradford, and first became interested in coaching. By the time he earned a master's degree in 1961, he had grown strongly attached to MSU—much like his earlier attachment to Detroit Western during his formative years of development. "It was always, 'Do or Die for Western High!'" recalls Rankin, who is now the athletic director at Birmingham Groves High School. "We went to school plays, dances, anything at the school that was happening. We just wanted to be at the school."

Perles just wanted to be at MSU, even when he was directing the Steel Curtain defense that led Pittsburgh to four Super Bowl titles in the 1970s. When MSU bought out his contract from the Philadelphia Stars in 1983, the path was cleared—and it looked as if he'd be there forever.

But in January 1990, for the second time in two years, Perles seemed perilously close to taking the money and running, this time to the Jets. For him to stay, MSU's Board of Trustees was forced to push through a vote to approve him as the school's new athletic director when Doug Weaver stepped down on July 1. Doing this, they ignored standard procedure for such a hiring process and merely scoffed at affirmative action guidelines. Without this widely criticized action by the board—which challenged and incensed MSU President John DiBiaggio— Perles probably would have left the school two which, two years earlier, he had pledged undying loyalty. And without the contract extension he received in 1988, he almost surely would have bolted for Green Bay at that time.

So where does loyalty come into it? And how strong is a love that has twice been superseded by lust? Perhaps the most powerful loyalty at MSU now is that of Spartan fans and supporters to Perles—a blind faith that he first seemed to understand that afternoon in January of 1988 and now seems rather adept at using for personal and financial gain. There is something inherently ill-intentioned about someone who will give and take away loyalty, who manipulates feelings with the sole objective of personal gain. Perles has done it twice, adding five years to his contract and the job of athletic director, simply by frightening important people with a very simple trick: threatening to leave for greener pastures.

But then, he has performed this psychological legerdemain before. Perles has always claimed a strong commitment to academics, even placing it ideologically ahead of football and victories and Rose Bowls in importance. On the surface, this rare ranking of priorities in a cutthroat profession is admirable. It's a belief he trumpets endlessly to new members of the media, attempting almost to brainwash by repetition. "Academics before football—that's the way it is here," he will boast. "If we don't win another game, so be it."

It's a worthy sentiment, but it misses the mark when student-athletes aren't given the proper time to vigorously pursue a degree. It is another contradiction, one that will be examined more closely in a subsequent chapter. Perles was hired to win football games, not to spearhead a reorganization of healthy priorities. He is a football coach, a tough disciplinarian, who demands extreme effort and time on the practice field. He brought the strict regimentation of the pros, previously absent from East Lansing, and put it in place immediately. Instead of 90-minute workouts, practices would sometimes last more than three hours. Summers weren't a time for relaxation, but rather hours to be spent in the weight room. It was indeed a culture shock for the players. "He used to practice us for so long," former Spartan quarterback Dave Yarema recalls. "You used to be just miserable wondering, 'Why are we out here?' After a while, you begin to think it's a negative instead of a positive. But playing in the fourth quarter sometimes, you could see where that practice time paid off."

The message was clear: The relaxed atmosphere of the Muddy Waters era wouldn't be tolerated. One former athlete, Craig Johnson, said Perles' NFL-type intensity automatically placed football above outside interests, including academics. "They expected so much from you that football was always first," says Johnson, who came to MSU in 1984 and still had not graduated by the summer of 1990. "I mean, that's why you're there—to play football."

Perles was there to return the Spartan program to national prominence. So when he first walked into the Duffy Daugherty Football Building and found players coming off a 2-9 season wearing less-than-respectable clothes, without a workout schedule, lacking the discipline of most high school squads, he felt things had to change. And they did. "Guys who were hangers-on or just getting by under

Muddy could not deal with the regimen and discipline Perles brought to the program," says former Spartan center Pat Shurmur, the first recruit of Perles' inaugural recruiting class in 1983. "Some of the guys couldn't deal with it and ended up leaving, and those who didn't fit into the program were just cast aside. There was a drastic difference about what Perles was about and what Muddy was about."

In fact, the two were total opposites. Waters nurtured his football background at places like Hillsdale College and Saginaw Valley State; Perles was an assistant under the tradition-rich Duffy Daugherty and the Steelers. Waters addressed the team wearing green and white sweats; Perles donned a suit and tie. The differences in the men ultimately created a difference in environment and attitude. "Muddy would show up in green and white, and the players would just take advantage of this Santa Claus figure," says Lynn Henning, who covered the team's transition for the Detroit *News.* "George would come in and chew guys out for the way they dressed. He let them know the party was over. The chaos of the Muddy Waters era cannot be overemphasized. It was a case of the inmates running the asylum."

Former Spartan linebacker Tim Moore, another member of Perles' first recruiting class, offers an equally graphic evaluation of those left over from the Waters program. "It took George time to weed out all the losers," he said. "And there were a bunch of losers. They were the kind of losers who didn't care about winning football games. There'd be guys drunk or on drugs during practice."

But even the straight ones, the ones who cared, felt the effects of Perles' win-at-all-costs, pro-football mentality. "There were old-timers who were good enough to play who got pushed aside by guys recruited by Perles," recalls Mark Kaczmarek, a Spartan offensive lineman from 1980

to 1983. The new coach would win it his way, with his
players. Perles' 1983 class consisted of a mind-boggling
33 recruits, from which he selected those who fit his idea
of a football player. The rest didn't last long, no matter
what their academic aspirations or how much they cared.
How could anything other than football have mattered? It
was basically a professional mini-camp, that August meat
market that set the tone for the Perles era. If you were
good enough on the field, you became a part of the
program. If not, you would be phased out to create space
for another scholarship.

"There are guys who aren't productive who, in essence,
are mistakes," Shurmur said. "Sooner or later, they'll
realize that and leave on their own. Perles had 33 scholarships to give, so he gave 33 scholarships. That was
because of the changing of the guard. The guys who were
Muddy's boys got run out. And out of the 33, we had more
guys who couldn't produce, so they left."

Perles' dealings with the media are sometimes just as
crude. Since he cares so deeply about bringing the program to national prominence—and keeping it there scan-
dal-free—any negative suggestions in the media are
greeted with direct and personal resentment. Like a
mother bear protecting her young, Perles will step in
front of any danger or controversy his players may be
confronted with and personally challenge the source
itself. Most reporters learn quickly that the way to secure
access to Perles and his players is to gloss over or ignore
issues that are sure to irritate the man providing the
access.

Some don't, however, and the criticisms they make of
the program soon return in the form of Perles' personal
and vindictive abuse. A case in point is Tim Staudt, a
sports anchor for WILX-TV in Jackson. "You know why I
always give him a recommendation for other jobs?" Perles

once asked a print reporter. "So I can get him the hell out of here."

Detroit *News* sports editor Joe Falls recalls being yelled at in Perles' office for a full half-hour before the tirade finally ended when Falls began laughing. Indeed, nearly every writer who has covered Spartan football has similar tales of Perles' intimidation behind closed doors. It comes with the territory when you work with a man who lives by the law of the street—where criticisms are delivered in person, and with fists. The personal affront doesn't begin immediately. Perles tries to mold each new reporter who enters the building, but questions eventually arise. At some point, particularly when his players come up against the law, questions must be asked.

Perles understands that. But he doesn't provide answers; he habitually pleads the notion that the team is his family, and that family matters are private. "This is family," Perles will protest. "We don't do our laundry in the street."

Unless, of course, he chooses to do so. Then private squabbles become public fodder. He pleads for privacy when football matters are concerned, but the moment enough hatred for a particular writer overflows, Perles forgets about his previous policy. He waits for an un-suspecting forum—usually his weekly press conference—and wields his angry sword once again in the name of his beloved university. And the attacks aren't limited to literary criticism. They get personal. In 1987, Perles took exception to a Falls column and launched a five-minute rampage. "Joe Falls is a loser," he told about 50 of Falls' peers.

The crescendo of bitterness erupted on November 25, 1989. The Spartans had just wrapped up a bid to the Aloha Bowl with a win at Wisconsin, and the post-game questioning was nearing an end. Then came the atomic explosion. Figuring tailback Blake Ezor still had a ten-day jail term to serve that December, Detroit *News* sportswriter Dave Dye inquired about Ezor's availability for the trip. A vicious verbal assault followed. Embarrassed cameramen turned off their lights. Red-faced reporters switched off their tapes. Veterans of Perles' bullish tactics concur that such rifts should be handled behind closed doors, but in this case the doors weren't closed—Perles did his laundry in the street.

Dye: "Is Blake going to be able to leave with the rest of the team to Hawaii?

Perles: "Yeah, Blake's going to be able to leave. Yeah, get that, Dave. You could take a good f———day and make a problem out of it. Why don't you wait until Monday? You must be the lowest that's ever worked in the business. Why don't you let the kids have five minutes before you start looking for dirt? You're a professional at it. Yeah, he's going to be all right and he'll be able to play. You want to ask a follow-up on it?"

Dye: "No, I've got everything I need."

Perles: "You make me . . (he pauses) . . You're an embarrassment to your profession. I'm sick of you and the things you look for. You couldn't have a good time if it were Christmas. I'm glad I had this opportunity to say this. You got a follow-up? Get it off your chest, and then you can go look for more dirt and write it any way you want. I'm sick of you. How's your problem? Is your problem OK? Are you in good shape? Are you going to your meetings?"

The final comment referred to Dye's battle with gambling, a problem that surfaced while he covered the Detroit Pistons. When Perles caught wind of the story, he used it as ammunition to question Dye's integrity behind his back. He discussed the topic often with other writers in private, but now Perles had made it public. And he had done it in brutal fashion.

It was a slip-up by Perles, a regression to a time when public displays of unbridled aggression were the norm. He is commonly characterized as a typical 1950s Detroit product—a tough kid who lived through social Darwinism in a tough town—but perhaps that assessment is too easy. While Perles' fiery temperament may have been accentuated by the environment in and around Detroit Western, its roots were deep within the gifted football, baseball, and hockey player who lived life hard.

"He was the best lineman to come out of that area for a while, and it wasn't because of his size," said Sam Eliowitz, former Detroit Chadsey athletic director and Western's quarterback during Perles' senior year. "It was his mental set. He was a tough, aggressive kid, and that may have been the reason that a lot of people might not have liked him. But he took his toughness and his overbearing attitude and he made something out of himself. For a while it didn't look like he was going to do that. It looked like he might be going to jail."

Indeed, Perles' frequent tendency to drink and fight (almost always in that order) led some people to believe that his aggression stemmed from more than his early environment. "I don't think you had to fight to survive, but George did anyway," Eliowitz said. "He would get a little drunk and then he'd be looking for a fight. That would happen quite a lot."

Eliowitz remembers attending a party where Perles was flicking a light switch on and off before finally being asked to stop. Taking the order personally, Perles asked his adversary to step outside. "They had a big audience," Eliowitz recalls, "and George shouted out that the cops were coming. Well, the guy turned around to look and George sucker-punched him and started kicking him on the ground."

There are times now when Perles probably would love to play by the same rules—in an animalistic, fight-to-the-death arena—but realizes it isn't at all possible. After tearing up his knee against Wisconsin in 1958, it became evident that coaching would be his only contribution to football. With the guidance of Eddie Rutherford, who coached him at Western and is now his administrative assistant, Perles tried hard to tone down his vindictive aggressiveness to levels suitable for a coach or teacher.

"Without any athletic outlet, he totally submerged himself in coaching," Eliowitz said. "Eddie told him there were no secrets to coaching, you just had to burn the midnight oil. And I think that's been his philosophy throughout his career. He is still very strong, very aggressive."

Those attitudes inevitably carry over to the football field. "Mainly, George is a tough coach," says Tim Moore, a former Spartan linebacker, "and he can gain the respect of a tough player." Part of that process is challenging the player himself. It happened often, and Moore recalls one particular instance when a fight broke out between two MSU players at practice: "I was standing there watching and someone pushed me from behind. I gave the guy an elbow and then turned around and it was George. He grabbed me and started hitting me. He said, 'You want to fight? You fight me! You fight me!'"

Perles must have realized this volatile nature would have to be cooled if he were to be perceived as an able leader. He must have known he had to do it. He had dreams of affluency, dreams of success, and those grandiose aspirations—which if they were realized at all would be realized under public scrutiny—required change. Changes of the heart? Perhaps, or maybe Perles internalized aggressions and prejudices that were too much a part of him to forget. When he screams at a reporter at frightening volume or speaks of avenging small personal harms, perhaps it is a portion of this forbidden rage begging to be released. A discussion of these psychological dynamics—which are admittedly guessed-at—is not intended as a judgment of George Perles, but rather as a means of gaining a better understanding of a complex man whose true nature we may never see.

♦ ♦ ♦

He entered through the back door, his head sunk down and hands dug deep in his pockets—a solemn entrance for a solemn night. The dark shadows beneath Dr. John DiBiaggio's eyes were never more pronounced, and perhaps never more meaningful. The Michigan State president laid down his papers and gently leaned against the back wall. Then he peered out into the row of cameras to see what the system had wrought.

For it was in this crowded Lincoln Room in the Kellogg Center, a usually tidy area suited for 100—which needed this night to hold 400 passionate observers—that it would all end: The speculation, the infighting, the power struggle, the search for a new athletic director.

It was also the night Michigan State University's reputation as an academic institution crumbled. Perhaps not completely, but it certainly cracked. And George Perles, who had triumphantly walked into a similar room two years earlier to proclaim he was staying forever, was curiously absent. The source of the apocalypse was nowhere to be seen.

The fall from grace came in the form of an emergency MSU Board of Trustees meeting. What exactly the term "emergency" meant depended on which side you stood, or on how much you valued a winning football team.

Trustee Larry Owen called the meeting to offer Perles the dual job of athletic director/football coach on a one-year trial basis. Perles had flown home from negotiations with the New York Jets on Long Island the night before. The Jets were hanging a five-year, multimillion-dollar contract in the coach's face, and Owen and others felt Perles would bite unless quick action was taken. Besides, this newest fascination with the pros cut dangerously into the heart of recruiting season. Something had to be done. And fast.

But the majority of the crowd packed the place for another reason, and it wasn't to worship at the shrine of the athletic department. Unlike the Crossroads scene, there were no pats on the back here—just anger and fear. They feared the university was about to become like all the other revenue-hungry sports institutions that merely dabble in academia. A vote for Perles, a vote to forego a complete search to replace Weaver, a vote against the warnings and protestations of DiBiaggio, they believed, would forever singe the school's spirit and image.

So the crowd crammed into this plush, powder-blue room to see if it were real. It certainly didn't appear to be. Indeed, it appeared simple. Affirmative action and academic integrity must be worth more to the school than football games.

They weren't.

A full media crush—complete with more cameras than normally appear at Saturday games at Spartan Stadium—was there to document it. The rumor mill had been in full gear since Perles confirmed that on December 24 he had been contacted by Jets General Manager Dick Steinberg as the Spartans prepared for a Christmas Day date in the Aloha Bowl. And where there are rumors, inevitably there will be media moguls as well.

To be honest, the participants in this scenario weren't exactly shy around reporters. From the very start, Michigan State University's search for an athletic director had been in the public eye. And everyone—the coach, the president, and the trustees—had campaigned for their positions in the papers. "This whole thing was botched," trustee Kathy Wilbur admitted afterward. The insanity began moments after the final seconds ticked away in the Aloha Bowl. With the Spartans leaving the field as 33-13 victors, here was Perles greeting an ABC interviewer and a national television audience with the following victory speech: "There's not an opening available now, but if there is one I'll be interested."

Less than 24 hours later, there would be. The New York Jets fired Joe Walton and Perles was hot property. DiBiaggio, knowing the coach's interest in the athletic director's job, was willing to let him slip away to the professional ranks. "I don't think we would bind him to a contract. We certainly don't want him to go. It's a matter of whether one might want to coach at a university or in the pros."

The president, of course, underestimated the intoxicating thrill of a winning football program. And if Perles wanted to stay, then trustee Larry Owen was going to fight for him. That meant naming Perles athletic director, whether he was qualified or not. Owen tried rounding up votes on the eight-person board—five would keep Perles no matter what the president thought.

DiBiaggio was overmatched.

The mutiny wasn't immediate. The board still questioned in mid-January, as the president did, whether one man could hold the position of football coach and athletic director. But when the Newark *Star Ledger* reported on January 19 that Perles would sign with the Jets, the pace quickened. The Detroit *News* said two days later that he would sign a five-year, $6 million contract, and the board panicked. A private meeting didn't produce the five votes needed, but they would come the next day, January 22, as Perles negotiated with Steinberg in Hempfield, New York. The board was prepared to offer Perles the athletic director's job on a one-year trial basis. That was all Perles needed to hear: he flew back to East Lansing as king of the campus. "I've tried to be honest and up front all the way through," he said the next morning on WJR radio's *J.P. McCarthy Show.* "That's all I've ever tried to do."

But it wouldn't be easy. In fact, Perles' name would be trampled harder than after any loss. His much-talked-about loyalty was questioned and the campus was outraged. Students gathered on the Wells Hall bridge to protest the victory of athletics over ethics. Some of them showed up to address the board at the Tuesday night emergency meeting, but it hardly mattered. It was a done deal.

Nevertheless, it was a spirited fight. Thirteen of the 14 persons who requested to speak supported DiBiaggio. One—a representative of the Downtown Coaches Club, the football program's boosters program—encouraged what the board was about to do. He was lustily cheered by the 50 or so players who had gathered at the back of the room.

But it was DiBiaggio, in what many consider his finest moment, who drew the most applause. He delivered an emotional message, one he had spent the entire night before creating. "The institution's credibility in the future could be in jeopardy. In essence, we denied, not encouraged, equal opportunity to potential candidates. I am extremely disappointed at that denial. And I am concerned a message has been sent nationally that intercollegiate athletics is an area set apart from institutional goals, commitments, and values at Michigan State University.

"I do not consider this a personal affront," he continued, "but as one that could in the long run hurt the university far more than the loss of any coach, any recruit, or any game."

The crowd cheered, but it wouldn't last. Here was Michigan State, nearly 14 years to the day after the NCAA slapped the football program with a three-year probation, toiling in dangerous waters once again. Larry Owen would set the tone of the board's vote: "Seven years ago we had a 2-9 football team. George Perles has brought back respect." Trustee Robert Weiss added, "The last ten years it's been fun to call yourself a Spartan."

So much fun that trustee Kathy Wilbur, the deciding vote, said yes and the resolution to save George passed, 5-3. "I wanted to protect the stability of the program," she said.

Meanwhile, the rest of the university shuddered. DiBiaggio threatened to resign, while trustees, students, and alumni loathed the decision. Dean Pridgeon, the leading trustee against Perles, feared for the future. "It elevated athletics, particularly football, to a spot up above the university," he said after the vote. "I thought this school was above that."

Many others thought so too, and the outrage came from all over. WXYZ-TV announcer Bill Bonds delivered perhaps the most profound response: "What kind of man or woman will MSU get as its next president? Top notch or maybe something less? Probably something less. The next highly qualified, bright Ph.D., a person dedicated to education, will have to face a brutal fact—at Michigan State University, in East Lansing, Michigan, football is king, academics a necessary prince-in-waiting behind the king's throne."

Bonds wasn't alone in his analysis. Even the sportscasting community supported DiBiaggio. Bob Reynolds, a Detroit radio announcer for close to 50 years and the voice of Spartan football for 18, lambasted the board for its decision. "I have never been so ashamed of my university in my entire life. It's a sad day."

"When will the university recover?" someone asked.

"It may take more years than I'll ever be around, I'm sure." Reynolds replied. "This has become the laughingstock of higher education in the country."

With that, people began filing out. The teachers cursed, the students shrugged, and the athletic boosters—with their "Keep a Spartan at MSU" buttons—left in a jovial mood. The voting was done, and Perles was staying. There would be a good recruiting class after all.

Lost in all the commotion and celebration was the president's future. Many feared he would leave East Lansing because of the rift. "It scares me," Pridgeon said. "If I were in his position, I'd have the resumés out tomorrow."

Yet DiBiaggio didn't indicate any move to leave. At his February State of the University Address, DiBiaggio announced plans to make the athletic department more accountable in relation to academics. Still, the president didn't meet with his new athletic director until four months after the vote, and it became increasingly clear that he and Perles weren't working on the same page.

"When I met with him initially, I told him he'd have to be evaluated in terms of public relations skills, his financial responsibility," DiBiaggio said. "These are not necessarily measured in a coach—they're two different kinds of roles. So I don't know."

Does anybody?

♦ ♦ ♦

The human soul can be driven by a number of things. Greed. Ego. Power. Only George Perles knows for sure which, if any, of those evils played a role in his latest brush with the NFL. In the bruising aftermath of Perles' selection as athletic director, each was blamed for bending the coach's immense loyalty to his alma mater. As indicated earlier, a special bond to Michigan State has not been the primary force behind his business decisions. Loyalty, after all, isn't something tangible. It's an effective form of propaganda that can easily be thrown about, depending on the situation or mood.

There has been another, more realistic thread woven throughout Perles' seven-year stay at MSU: security. It has been a basis for thought and action his entire career—whether it was security in jobs, finances, or media coverage. He doesn't like surprises, especially where his future is concerned. "The guy was always coming up with plans," says Dave Yarema, a quarterback under Perles from 1983 to 1986. "He would have a plan for a plan." This doesn't explain why the MSU sideline often appears in complete disarray during crucial moments on offense, but that's another point. This deals with more than draw plays.

Much of Perles' youth involved financial uncertainty. His Lithuanian father, Julius, worked in payroll for Ford Motor Company and never even dreamed of attaining a college degree. It was not even part of the scene. Indeed, Perles was the first in his family to graduate from high school. "Very few of the guys in the old neighborhood ever went to college," says Bill Rankin. "What you would usually do is get whatever kind of job your father had. College was a method of escape. It was a way out for George. College certainly wasn't something that was shoved in his face as a five-year-old." So football meant a scholarship. Football meant money, opportunity, and hope. Even now, Perles' single objective—almost his obsession—is to provide adequately for his family. It's a noble thought.

Many object, however, that he has obtained that security in a rather ignoble manner. From day one, Perles began cultivating supporters within the Michigan State family: key board members, Governor James Blanchard, Attorney General Frank Kelley. Some refer to the clique as his power source, but it may be more accurate to describe the group as insurance. By wining and dining a select group of influential boosters, Perles made sure he would be given ample time to build a program. With the foundation successfully in place and the NFL beginning to show interest, that group now insures that Michigan State will consider him indispensable and attempt to top any offer—whether it's a pay raise, an extension of his contract, or, as we have seen, a promotion. It's no coincidence that each time Perles strayed a bit to listen to the pros, the ante was raised. And his stronghold on financial security tightened another notch.

"He really did a good job of cementing his security," says Lynn Henning, formerly with the Detroit *News* and now an editor at *PGA Golf Magazine* in Troy. "He's a very insecure man. He wants to make sure he has everything covered. He is in love with money. Not that he's a big spender. He just wants to make sure his future is all wired up. He wants his nest egg built."

Perles may never again have a financial worry. His base salary is $123,000, and, beginning in 1993, he and his wife Sally will receive lifetime monthly payments of $3,750 from an annuity to which the university has contributed greatly. Pile on revenue attained through an extensive speaking tour and profits from his privately owned television show, and the Perles family has a secure economic foundation for the future. In fact, Perles reports his football-related income as $325,000 annually.

But with the financial headache erased, there exists a new one—silencing the critics. Never before has Perles' character and ability been questioned more. The athletic director fiasco has led to enormous criticism, some justified, some cruel. The five trustees who passed the resolution have received the brunt of the blows, but a good number have been directed at Perles as well. After all, he was the one who pressed the issue and, in the end, was given the job before a single other candidate was considered.

Throughout the mess, Perles looked puzzled. He truly doesn't understand the storm of anger. He sees himself as a loyal MSU man who was promoted and will work hard for his school. Others realize that Perles has no previous administrative experience and wasn't even interviewed to discover if he had any of those skills, and that's the major worry. Perles is a football coach. Always has been, and always will be. True, he may be able to delegate authority well, but an athletic director must deal with financial and legal issues, direct and fund the school's 25 other sports, and make time for the coaches. Not to mention that he will also be football coach, an overwhelming position in itself. How hospitable will Perles be when, say, the volleyball coach calls with a crisis during the heat of recruiting season? We'll see.

The point is, it's not an X's and O's job. Doug Weaver has a law degree. Perles has a master's degree in physical education. The two aren't compatible. Consider the following interview concerning the amount of money the athletic department makes from the average football game. When we spoke with him, Perles was sitting in his office, stumbling over the most basic of administrative questions, moments before taking off on a speaking tour that would take him from Grand Rapids to Montreal. It was eight months before he was to become the school's new athletic director.

Q: How much gate do you get in from a full stadium on average?

Perles: Yeah, I can do that for you. I think I'm capable of this. *(He pulls out a calculator and slowly pecks each number.)* OK, 76,000 times $18 equals, well, looks to me like $1,368,000 a game if you take 18 times 76.

Q: Then you have concessions, or is that . . .

Perles: I don't know about this. I don't know if some guys get discounts. I don't know.

Q: So $18 is the average each person pays?

Perles: That's what a ticket costs.

Q: Yeah, but students don't pay $18.

Perles: I don't know what they pay.

Q: I think they pay $8. Anyway, this isn't very scientific.

Perles: Well, f— off. *(He laughs.)* How many students are there? Let's go 60,000 times $18 equals

$980,000. 16,000 times $18 equals $288,000. Hot
dogs. How much do hot dogs cost? How the f— do
I know? But I'll try. I don't know how much they
make. *(He pauses and smirks.)* I know how much
I make.

Those familiar with the school's turmoil-filled history
see Perles' promotion as an invitation for trouble.

"He isn't an athletic director," challenges Henning, a
1974 MSU graduate. "He isn't any more capable of being
an athletic director than I am of becoming a nuclear
scientist. It's the most absurd and ridiculous event I've
seen happen up there—and that's saying something. When
it happened, I said, 'Get ready. There's either going to be
an NCAA probe or a financial scandal.' I can't believe it
took less than ten days to happen. But that's what they
are going to end up with. It was a short-sighted, idiotic
move."

Shortly after the board's vote, Spartan booster J.D.
Anderson claimed Perles sold seats on the team plane in
exchange for $2,500 worth of advertising on his weekly
TV show. Perles dismissed the story, charging that Anderson frequently arrived for flights intoxicated and insulted
players.

But just weeks later, Grand Rapids businessman
George Byam concurred with Anderson's testimony concerning Perles' monetary bully tactics. Byam, whose jewel-
ry company made rings for Spartan athletes, claims Perles
threatened to take his business elsewhere unless Byam
paid $2,000 for the show. "What distresses me," Byam
said from his Grand Rapids home, "is here was a guy using
his position to basically enrich himself by threatening to
withhold public business." Perles, of course, denied using
extortion to help his pocketbook. But that doesn't
surprise Byam, who questions Perles' credibility. "I expect
him to say that," Byam said. "He stonewalls like that on a
lot of issues. And it works very nicely for him. He thinks

the world revolves around him." The aspersions may be just the first of many to hit the Perles era.

And that's too bad. In a quiet moment, Perles once reflected on his life, a storybook trek that delivered him from the depressed streets around Vernor Highway to a lifetime toiling in the field he loves most—football. Most mortals should be so fortunate. "You know, I'm the luckiest guy in the world," he said, glancing at his office wall and the faces of people like Biggie Munn, Duffy Daugherty, and Chuck Noll. "What would I be if I weren't a football coach? I'd be a high school phys ed teacher somewhere teaching volleyball. But here I am. I'm a football coach." And he's a good one. Not great, not legendary, but good.

No one really knows how history will judge George Perles at his new profession. Perhaps he will do just fine. But it also could prove to be a tragic non sequitur for Perles, who dreams of being a Green and White legend like his mentors, especially Duffy. His intense desire for security, his unrelenting need for assurance that the next athletic director will continue to emphasize his program, may have set the stage for his greatest downfall. Now, the nation watches, and his name and school may have been stained forever. It's a fact that may return to haunt Perles.

"You never get hurt by knocks from outside people," he said prior to the controversy. "The only time they hurt is when they are internal. Michigan State's never been hurt from the outside. The only time Michigan State's had problems is when there has been internal fighting."

2

THE STUDENT-ATHLETE

"Academics first, family second, football third."

– George Perles

It is difficult to feel bitterness toward someone who unknowingly hurts others, whose naïveté or weak grasp of right and wrong is the fault either of society or of fostering influences.

But when someone who understands society's values and laws still uses tools of manipulation to further his own ends, we feel vulnerable and let down. We feel used.

George Perles hands out pieces of idealistic rhetoric like penny candy. He pays lip service to the heroic and laudable values held most dear, especially on a university campus, like academic excellence and domestic tranquility and respect for one's fellow man. But he does this in the face of the realization that these ideals may at times conflict with the demands of running a big-time football program. Still, Perles insists on the best of both worlds. He will have a winning football program on a national scale, he insists, and he will do it without sacrificing

27

academic integrity, personal and family responsibilities, or respect for other people and for authority.

This seemingly wonderful fantasy, his Utopian gridiron, begins to erode as the hypocrisy of "academics first, family second, football third" becomes too obvious to ignore or deny.

◆ ◆ ◆

Steve McCornack, a communications professor at Michigan State, first heard from Greg Croxton by phone the week before fall term finals in December 1989. Croxton, a former Spartan player, is Perles' academic advisor. "That's pretty loosely construed," offers McCornack. "I find it rather ironic that he has that title."

Croxton contacted McCornack on behalf of MSU tailback Blake Ezor, who had been convicted of a second-offense impaired driving violation on August 7, 1988. More than one year later (September 27, 1989), Ezor was sentenced to serve ten consecutive days in jail, but the judge kindly gave him until December 27 to serve the sentence so he could complete fall term classes. "He can't miss ten days of school," Perles said at the time. "That's why the judge gave him the sentence he did. It makes sense to me."

But it somehow made less sense after the Spartans were invited to the December 25 Aloha Bowl. For Michigan State University's starting tailback to make all the practices leading up to the game, he would have to be out of jail by Saturday, December 9. That obviously would require him to be in the Mason, Michigan facility at the time his Thursday, December 7 final exam was given in McCornack's required Communications 350 class.

Ezor's final exam would have to be either missed or moved back for him to get out of jail in time to make all the Aloha Bowl practices, and that prompted a phone call from Croxton.

"He said, 'Here's the deal. Blake has decided he's going to serve his jail term during finals week. Can you give him an incomplete in your COM 350 class so he can make up the work?'" recalls McCornack. "I said there was no way I was going to give him an incomplete. Incompletes are given to students with an illness or a death in the family, and then only when they've been in good standing up to that point. Blake had hardly shown up for class."

So Ezor (who was in even worse shape in COM 460, which met at the same time as COM 350) was faced with a rather difficult decision. However, this was far from a personal matter—a fact that became quite evident when Croxton placed his first phone call to McCornack. This was not a Blake Ezor problem. This was a football problem.

The options were clear, then, when Perles, Croxton, and Ezor met in Perles' office around 6:00 p.m. on the afternoon of November 29 to discuss their plan of action: football or academics?

It wasn't even close.

Ezor arrived at Rick's American Café, an East Lansing bar, while the bouncers were flicking on the lights and pleading with stragglers at 2:00 a.m. on Thursday, November 30. Visibly intoxicated, he talked of beginning his sentence that very morning, but he says now he didn't become a prisoner until 5:00 p.m. "It was a last-minute decision is what it was," he said, and at that time he was still under the false impression that he would receive incompletes from his professors and make up the work.

When Croxton was contacted three days later and asked about Ezor's sudden incarceration, he replied that he was surprised to hear such news and that he knew nothing about the situation. "Blake must have done it on his own," he said.

Perles, meanwhile, told reporters that Ezor's academic well-being was both considered and intact. "The important thing was to make sure his finals were all covered," he said.

Despite these falsehoods, Perles and Croxton still clung to the narrow and naïve hope that everything would work out fine. Croxton had called McCornack on Thursday, November 30, the day Ezor went to jail, and informed him that Ezor definitely would miss his final on the following Thursday. "He apparently needed to successfully complete one class that term to stay eligible [for the game], but there was no way I was going to give him an incomplete," says McCornack, who recalls Croxton playing on his sympathies for half an hour.

The plan had been to eliminate the problem of the two simultaneous classes (COM 350 and COM 460) swiftly and covertly. Ezor, through Croxton, would take an incomplete in McCornack's 350 class and drop 460, which he hadn't attended once. "But then they said, 'This McCornack's gonna be a hard ass,'" says McCornack. So Croxton decided he might try dropping that class and taking an incomplete in 460. But David Kragt, head of undergraduate affairs for the department, said there was "no way in hell" they were going to take an incomplete in a class they had been trying to drop since two weeks into the term.

So Croxton called McCornack again on Friday, December 1, and said there was no problem, everything was fine. Ezor would take the makeup final on Friday, December 8, the last day of finals week—and also the day he would be released from jail, after serving nine days instead of ten. McCornack, who thought that was "kind of mysterious," didn't see how Ezor could possibly pass but said he'd let him take it. "After a while," says McCornack, "it felt like I was punishing Ezor for something Croxton had done."

Ezor was oblivious to these academic struggles and to the outside world in general. He had enough on his mind trying to prove his manliness to fellow prisoners, who found his flowing blond hair and glamorous football life-style suitable reasons to question it. He fought a black inmate over a television show. He put up with constant verbal abuse and found prison life "too crazy to study." And he waited.

When he was released, on Friday, December 8, Ezor discovered a message from Croxton on his answering machine at home: "Get your butt over to McCornack's office and take your final."

The makeup final was given to McCornack's other students at 1:00 p.m. Ezor showed up at three.

"It was understood that I'd be able to make up my exams," recalls Ezor, who later referred to McCornack as a "little f——." "But then he refused to give me my exam because I had gone to jail. He said, 'You shouldn't have gone to jail. You should have taken your finals and missed football, because school was more important.'"

Ezor asked if he could just fill in a test grid sheet at random, hoping to get enough answers right by sheer chance to pass the exam. At that point, McCornack began to weaken. "I saw Blake as the victim and Croxton as the bad guy," he said. "I didn't want to feel sorry for Blake, but I did. I mean, I was starting to feel like a jerk. It was just starting to register for him that I wasn't going to let him take the test."

In the end, McCornack's decision came down to two factors: 1) he wouldn't have given anyone else such a break, and 2) Ezor, however indirectly, had made a decision to sacrifice finals in favor of football.

"He said, 'It's all your decision,'" recalls McCornack. "And I told him my answer was no."

Ezor contends that McCornack had it in for him and had never liked him, but the decision was, in fact, an extremely difficult one made by a man torn between sympathy and principle.

McCornack reasons that Ezor could have begun his jail sentence—which turned out to be nine days long—the day after his COM 350 final exam, and have been released on December 16. Michigan State's flight to Honolulu didn't leave until December 18, but that would have caused Ezor to miss a week of practice time.

"I don't think the guy's going to finish his degree," says McCornack, who points out that Ezor would need a 4.0 average in his class next time he takes it just to obtain a passing grade. "These players are just one injury away from having nothing if they don't get their degree. What's Blake going to do, go back to Vegas and deal cards?

"Perles talks about academics first, school second, and football third. What a bunch of crap. It really pisses me off what Croxton is trying to do, and he isn't operating on his own. Perles is the one orchestrating it. It was highly unethical and probably illegal. Blake can't help it; he's a genetic freak. They were just running him through the system. He's a tiny little guy who can run like hell, but he's the victim of a system that puts football as its main priority. What a cheap deal. Perles told the media that it wouldn't affect Blake's academic standing, but it did. It did."

♦ ♦ ♦

Ezor will not graduate from Michigan State University anytime soon, but that is not a calamity that presently wears on his mind. When a kid has been instructed for five years that football is the answer, that football is life, misadventures in the classroom are of secondary importance. Such misguided lessons are taught early on by Perles and his staff at MSU; the very structure of the program is geared toward keeping players eligible. This entails channeling a "student-athlete" into a major course of study that is easy to pass, but not necessarily easy to master. The process of learning or elevating one's intellectual level is rarely considered. Perles, through Croxton, simply expects his players to reach an academic plateau that is considered acceptable by the NCAA.

The notion that the football program is subordinate to the academic program is a facade that begins with the first recruiting visit. Perles' rather substantial presence as an NFL assistant with the Pittsburgh Steelers, and his subsequent connections with the professional ranks, are neatly intertwined with any scholastic pitch that he may serve up to prospective recruits. This presents an interesting contradiction. On one hand, Perles is peddling a life filled with fame's wonderful spoils, a life in which running and passing aren't necessarily contingent upon obtaining a college degree. On the other hand, he speaks of an illusory academic priority that actually may get in the way of the first goal.

Perles often boasts of placing seven MSU players in the NFL draft's first round the last seven years. Dangling a dangerous carrot like that can place false hopes and dreams in the mind of a 17-year-old who, like most kids, has little chance of reaching such a low-percentage goal. "It would be dangerous if he did that," says Pat Shurmur, a former Spartan center who served as a graduate assistant under Perles while working on a master's degree and who is now the MSU tight ends coach. "But to be fair to him, I've never heard him do it."

Shurmur wasn't at Craig Johnson's house in early 1984. The highly touted tailback from Washington High in Massillon, Ohio welcomed a host of recruiters that winter. But one, boasting of an inside route to the NFL, made an impact. Michigan State assistant coach Nick Saban cited Perles' long resumé of professional experience, and Johnson was hooked.

"That was the first thing out of his mouth, and that was the major reason I wanted to go there," said Johnson, who unhappily left MSU without a degree in 1988 and who now works as a security guard at a Canton can company. "They talk about connections. You know, 'Perles has won four Super Bowls and we have this great reputation with the NFL. You come here and play and you'll get a shot.' That was a major, major recruiting method. He said that to a lot of kids. That's why he was getting all the players.

"That is misleading, but it's business. He's trying to keep his job and says what he says to get players in."

Such procedures, however effective, set a dangerous precedent before starry-eyed Spartans ever settle in at Case Hall, an MSU residence hall directly across from the Duffy Daugherty Football Building. If a coach wants you to come to his school because he can help you play professional football, doesn't professional football become, inevitably, the focus of your collegiate experience? Perhaps so, and it follows that your success on the Michigan State gridiron is the sole path to this promised land, which in actuality only one percent of collegiate players reach. As in Ezor's case, a choice between football and the classroom becomes a choice between an NFL shot and a much more deliberate path to prosperity. The NFL shot usually wins.

"All the athlete friends I knew never really talked about their subjects or schoolwork," recalls Johnson. "We just talked about sports. As freshmen and sophomores, we talked about football and the next team we were going to play. I can remember, during my senior year, wc started to talk about school a little more, because of the reality that it was going to end soon."

Of course, to play college football, a player must remain eligible. A highly recruited tailback who may not be a great student almost invariably will be placed in a major that simply allows him to play ball. Croxton has been known to strongly urge incoming student-athletes to major either in communications or criminal justice, instead of exploring their aptitude in other areas of study.

Take the 1987 Rose Bowl championship team. Of 40 student-athletes who played a significant role (more than 20 minutes) that season, 21 (53 percent) majored in either communications or criminal justice. Of those, 15 studied communications. Similarly, in 1988 13 of 22 starters on the team (59 percent) were majoring in one of those two areas, and nine were communications majors.

One of the signs of academic free-thinking in a football program is a wide range of majors among the players. Muddy Waters, who coached MSU from 1980 to 1982 before being fired because of a 10-23 record, had a 1981 starting squad which studied in 15 different areas. Perles' 1988 starters studied in six.

"Communications traditionally has been regarded as a blow-off degree," says McCornack, who taught the same subject at Illinois before coming to Michigan State. "It's an easy major to pass but not an easy major to excel in. There are a lot of people bumping along. There are a lot of bozos, a lot of idiots funneled in here by the athletic department."

Most communications classes are heavily populated, making enforcement of attendance next to impossible, McCornack says. The tests are often multiple choice, based solely on lectures, and it is possible for a student to receive a passing grade without even truly participating in the course.

This does not mean that achieving excellence as a communications major is not an admirable accomplishment. The field can be as challenging as any other to those who possess the time and inclination to pursue it aggressively.

Those who don't, often pass but learn little.

Some of these traits, of course, are true of other majors at Michigan State, but the area of communications has traditionally attracted athletes because it may aid a future broadcasting career. But only the students who apply themselves exceptionally ever get a real taste of what broadcasting entails. Too often, these students aren't athletes.

Eileen Van Tassell, an entomology professor at MSU and a member of the school's academic council, vividly remembers a career counseling session with a football player in January 1990. Specifically, she remembers being disturbed by it:

"What sort of subject interests you?"

"Well, I suppose I'll go into criminal justice."

"Is that what you're interested in, law enforcement, as a career?"

"No, not really. But that's what everybody says."

She shakes her head with the anguished frustration of one aware of a problem she alone can't remedy. It's a conversation she's had before. "The football program is not really helping him with what he needs in terms of career counseling. I was able to tell him more just sitting here in this office. I set up an appointment for him to get career counseling. Why isn't the football team doing that? Why?"

To Van Tassell, such a case suggests that key scholastic decisions at MSU are being treated lightly—and by someone other than the student-athlete.

"Are they pushed?" she asks herself. "Oh, yes. I can tell from just a few questions that I ask. Nobody ever sat down with them and suggested something they can do naturally and enjoy doing with their life. It's really a crime."

Even when student-athletes enter the program with career ideas outside football, those interests are soon crushed by the sport's heavy demands. Craig Johnson, for instance, was always fascinated by robotics. In order to play football, though, he traded in that fascination for an easier field of study—communications—and more time on the field.

"I thought I was going to be an engineer," he said. "That's what I wanted to do at college, you know. I always liked robotics. But the demands of football didn't give me enough time to study for it. So I changed to communications. A lot of guys went into communications, and I'm not saying they did it because it was easy. No degree is easy. But they went into it because a lot of the other guys would, and [advisors] would say, 'Come on, it's not so bad.'

"You would get frustrated that you couldn't take certain classes because of football. It's like, 'You say academics comes first, well, why can't I take this class?' They try to say they give you time for academics, but in actuality they don't. They make it look good. And maybe they even try, you know. But football is definitely first. It poses a problem."

This delicate balance of priorities is, for many, the first sign that football takes precedence at Michigan State University. Many players are so taken in by the adulation and celebrity status pervading major-college football that an inappropriate major means little or nothing. Examples are set from the top, and if coaches and media and alumni are telling players that beating Michigan is more important than working diligently toward a degree, of course those players are going to take the easy way out. Until the games are over, that is, when suddenly they're on their own.

"I think the attitude of the student-athlete has become worse as the income for athletics has skyrocketed all out of proportion to its value to society," Van Tassell says. "I tell them, 'Hey, you are playing a game. Don't lose sight of that. This is a game. Next year, nobody is going to care who won or lost. Nobody. Don't make yourself into a life-or-death person. You're not. You're an entertainer.

They come and go. Even the best of football players don't last long. Then what?'

"Some listen and some don't. I'm not sure to what extent the successful students are doing anything more than lip service. Some of them just sit there and watch. They get last-minute tutors and get through with a passing grade, and that's all they really care about."

Even if it means cheating. This is nothing new, really. It always has been an alluring option for student-athletes who, for one reason or another, haven't shown the same intensity in the classroom as on the field. Take the telling saga of Kirk Gibson, MSU's All-American football star who also had a knack for knocking baseballs clear out of Kobs Field. With his final year of football and a contract with the Detroit Tigers looming near, Gibson—with an overall grade point average of 1.6—enrolled in a class called "The History of American Sport," taught by history professor Peter Levine in the spring of 1978. "He came into class the first day to pick up the syllabus and I never saw him again," says Levine. "He missed his midterm so I figured that would be the end of him. But when it came time to turn in his paper, there was one about the commercialization of sport with his name on it."

There was a problem, though.

Levine remembered helping another baseball player, Larry Pashnick, several terms earlier on a similar assignment, which just happened to analyze the commercialization of sport. The paper Gibson turned in was Pashnick's. "So I failed him," Levine continues, "and I get a call on a Friday night. It was Kirk. He was going on and on about how an advisor had told him to take the class and not to worry. So I said, 'Get your ass in here Monday morning with a paper and we'll talk.'"

As it turned out, Gibson couldn't make that meeting. Instead, he was at Tiger Stadium that morning to sign a $200,000 contract. A profitable and certainly successful professional career was born. And Levine? He didn't turn Gibson in for plagiarism, but he did flunk the slugger. Looking back, Levine isn't bitter. "Who am I to tell him not to sign for all that money?"

While Gibson's lackadaisical attitude toward classroom responsibilities was a result of collegiate athletic prowess, at least he had a sound educational background from pre-college experience. Many aren't as lucky. Many have followed the sports-before-smarts doctrine for as long as they can remember.

To win football games, Perles and Michigan State University must accept some student-athletes who, without athletics, would not be considered university material—many of them from inner-city public school systems that are considered substandard. For these students, East Lansing is less of a learning center than a stepping stone on the road to professional football. This unfortunate perception is rarely challenged by the school's football program, so it usually never changes. Kids who don't study are told to pass. They rarely are told to think, to apply, to plan, to understand.

"It's a particular problem with the black kids in our cities, who are sold a bill of goods by this society—and I suspect it's endorsed by people like Perles—that football is their ticket to life," Levine says. "But for every Earvin Johnson, there are hundreds, maybe thousands, of these young people who never graduate."

That bill of goods is not surprising, given the influence that sports, and televised sporting events in particular, have in our society. While professional athletes can and often do return to inner-city high schools and preach the value of an education, it is difficult for the average 16-year-old athlete who can run like the wind to absorb this message. Beyond the rhetoric, he sees the crime and pain of a depressed neighborhood that has loomed outside his door every morning since birth. He then refocuses on the million-dollar athlete wearing his gold chains and expensive clothes and, for obvious reasons, that world entices him. College recruiters play on these dreams of fame and riches, especially when dealing with athletes living in economic despair. So when the reality of classrooms, books, and exams suddenly drops from the sky, the kid is already in a big hole.

"If a general lack of preparedness is a problem for some minority students, then the athlete suffers from it even more," says MSU history professor Harry Reed, who specializes in black studies. "In environments where the academics weren't that good to begin with, athletes just learn to get by. I've seen it. I've seen athletes who simply did not have a good high school experience. The skills were not there. And they don't have the time or the inclination to build those skills further. They are just interested in getting through the day and saving up energy for practice and getting through the week. They are at a real disadvantage."

When the game is no longer there, whether you're black or white, life is not nearly so grand. "A lot of the players have no imagination," says Professor McCornack. "I've seen guys who got injured and don't have a degree. They've got nothing. They were such assholes while they were playing that nobody can stand having them around anymore. All they can do is go flip burgers somewhere."

Pat Shurmur is the exception. After gaining his master's degree in financial administration, the cousin of Los Angeles Rams defensive coordinator Fritz Shurmur worked for IBM in Southfield, Michigan. He sees himself as lucky for having his academic priorities straight before he got to college. Too often, it's too late to change once you arrive.

"It's hard to concentrate on school," Shurmur says from the back booth of Kerby's, a Southfield restaurant. "Players see that, at arm's length, there are millions and millions of dollars. And they're 21 years old! So that accounting class, or that finance class, or learning about interest rates isn't that important. They kind of look past that, even when it's an important part of their development. I think that's the nature of the sport. Guys have been dreaming and dreaming about playing football, and they're three or four years away from being a professional athlete, potentially. So they see anything up to that time as sort of a holding period. Instead of using it productively, maybe they get their degrees, but they don't learn as much as they potentially could.

"In addition to moving from a place like Florida or Chicago into an atmosphere where you're put into major-college pressure, you've got a pile of dirty laundry and there are decisions to make, a growing-up process to go through, too. It gets a little overwhelming for guys."

There are, of course, success stories—players who consider their academic studies equally important as how many snaps they take in an afternoon, and who excel in both. People like Pat Shurmur and former safety Dean Altobelli, an honors student in mechanical engineering, represented the prototype student-athlete at Michigan State. Consequently, they were paraded around by Perles as examples of his commitment to education. "A Heisman would be nice, but I'd rather have a Rhodes scholar," Perles often boasted when Altobelli nearly won the renowned academic award in 1986. Perles' favorite ploy to stress his school sense would be to have such players stop by the football building on National Signing Day while he entertained the media. As Perles raved about the player's achievements in the classroom, the perception that followed was that the new recruits he was bringing in had the same intellectual and academic potential. It would be natural to think that, but also wrong. The Altobellis and Shurmurs are on the thin edge of a steep bell curve.

There also are those on the other end. Immense athletic specimens like recent Indianapolis Colts draft choice
Andre Rison, who hasn't passed sophomore status toward
a communications degree after four years of schooling,
don't feel compelled to attend class regularly, if at all.
They realize that as long as they stay eligible, they'll get
by and, most important, play football.

Between these two extremes is a huge group, student-
athletes who generally believe in the integrity of the system when they first arrive. Soon, however, they discover
the hypocrisy involved and must sacrifice either schoolwork or football and its million-dollar allure. Not
everyone follows the faint dream, though; some grow up.

◆ ◆ ◆

It took Mike Staisil nearly three years to see it, to
swallow the program's skewed priorities, and, finally, to
reject them. Staisil, slated to be a back-up offensive tackle
as a red-shirt sophomore in 1988, crumpled up his prep
All-American promise and threw it in the trash. Two
weeks before the season opener, the game ended and life
began. He quit the team. With seven different job offers
awaiting him when he graduated in June 1990, Staisil
says it was the best move of his life. "In high school, it was
fun. You had all your buddies and the whole school came
out to see you play. In college, it's a business—no question
about it. The revenue and profit they make off us is
unbelievable, and every year they bring in faster guys,
stronger guys like you wouldn't believe. It's just a big
business. Coach Perles wouldn't be here if it weren't. So
I just said, 'Hey, if I'm going to do this, I'm going to do it
right.'" Which meant the decision to drop football.

The six-foot-five, 246-pound lineman was a star at
Flint Central High School. He hung out with people like
former Central grad and current California Angels pitcher
Jim Abbott, and felt fulfilled within the world of athletics.

"You're considered a stud in high school," he explains. But Staisil was one of the lucky ones at Flint Central. Academics played an important part in his life—his father was a principal, his mother a teacher. Staisil managed to keep matters in perspective through all the high-fives, the practices, and the recruiting calls. His 3.85 grade point average and acceptance to several Ivy League schools are proof of that. He knew football was simply a game—or at least, he thought he knew it was.

Staisil arrived at Michigan State in August 1986 with the idea of graduating in three years. That thought changed in a hurry. "It wasn't as drastic as it was for some people, who never took academics seriously or who had a different type of background, but it still was tough," says Staisil, who majored in material logistics management. "Organization of time is the biggest thing. When you come up here, you're all gung-ho about football. You're putting a lot of time into it. And after football practice, it's not the easiest thing to pick up a book or do chemistry problems. It's hard. It's a different type of tiredness. Some are tired because they work at the library, or something else, but football makes you physically tired. It's different. They have study hall available at night, but some people just sit there and do very little, or make excuses for not going at all. I have a lot of friends who are communications majors, and I have nothing against that field, but it's the stereotypical major for athletes. It's a shame. I mean, there aren't going to be any interviewers coming to campus to talk to those guys."

Staisil shrugs and softens his stance somewhat. "But it's tough doing it around football. If you were hurt, even just a little bit, you had to get training at 7:00 a.m., whether you had a test to study for or whatever. They had your name on the list, so you had to be there. If you didn't show, then they'd say, 'You must not want to get better.'"

Still, Stasil managed to maintain an excellent grade point average—3.5 in the business school—throughout the madness. During the summer, while most of his teammates worked at landscaping jobs or put in endless hours in the weight room, Staisil opted for something else: an internship at General Motors Corporation in Flint, Michigan. A summer of Staisil sitting behind a desk didn't exactly appeal to the Spartan coaching staff, however. "They wanted me to stay down here and work out all summer. Finally, they said I could have the internship as long as I also worked out. So I started work at 6:00 a.m., worked until 4:30, and drove up here to lift, work out, and run. Sure, they want you to pursue some things in your major and your career, but there's a fine line there. You're on scholarship."

In other words, football came first, and that bothered Staisil. He knew the facts: Only one percent make the pros. The rest? There is a great giant scrap heap of former players out of work, without a degree, and with their eligibility expired. As training camp for the 1988 season began, Staisil wondered if he was going to wind up like all the rest. He decided he wouldn't let that happen.

"My experience at GM swung my thoughts," says Staisil, who later added a five-month internship at General Electric in 1989. "I said, 'This is great. I just got all this valuable experience, this is my field, and I love it.' So I'd be sitting in team meetings, and I was disinterested. I wasn't motivated. I was doing well, but it was getting kind of miserable. I knew I could stick it out for another two years and maybe have that shot at the pros but not have any hands-on business experience, or I could be well-rounded and make myself more marketable. So I figured, 'I have to pursue this more, because I'm not going to have the opportunities if I don't. I won't have as many job opportunities if I stick with football.'"

There is a tone of contentment, even boastfulness, in Staisil's words as he grabs a cheeseburger at P.T. O'Malley's, an East Lansing pub, reflects upon his past, and discusses his future. When he graduated, a job with a minimum annual salary of $35,000 awaited him. How many football players can say that? How many college graduates?

"So many people are just looking at the short-term angle of things," reasons Staisil, who says Perles was supportive of his decision. "A lot of kids come in for four years and then they're done. I just decided it was time to hang it up."

Even for those who excel within the student-athlete system, there is a resentment, a feeling that the dumb-jock syndrome touches one and all. Travis Davis, who arrived at Michigan State in 1985, would have been a Proposition 48 casualty if he had graduated from high school a year later, but he escaped that stigma and went on to excel academically. In addition to making All-Conference at his defensive tackle position, he gained a degree in merchandising management and was working on a master's degree during the 1989 season.

Four days before he played his final home game as a Spartan (on November 18, 1989, against Northwestern University), Davis rested his six-foot-three, 275-pound frame on the floor of the Duffy Daugherty Football Building and tried to sort out this whole student-athlete nonsense. A few weeks earlier, he had been arrested in connection with a brawl at a Lansing bar called Tango's, and the subsequent jock-bashing in the papers had clearly affected him. He didn't defend his actions, but he questioned whether the public fully understood the pressures placed upon football players at a major program.

"A lot of people get down on athletes because of the free ride they get," Davis said. "But the time spent and work put into being a student-athlete is more than the time spent by a lot of students. We have two jobs. It's not easy to practice for three hours and then go pick up a book. To knock someone senseless and then go study—well, you might think that person isn't all that bright."

He may not be realistic, either. This, after all, isn't fencing he is talking about. These players don't magically appear on Saturday afternoons, win ball games, travel to exotic Bowl appearances, and suffer through classes without an exorbitant amount of work. The sport doesn't leave these bodies when they walk off the practice field. The pinched nerves and strained muscles stay with them—through the film sessions, in the weight room, and out the door to class. It's not a game anymore; it has become a full-time occupation.

"It is," says Craig Johnson, agreeing with Davis' assessment. "It is holding two jobs, that's exactly what it is. You have a chance, but you can't possibly apply yourself fully to both academics and athletics. One is going to take from the other. It's almost impossible to do both at 100 percent."

Consider the schedule these student-athletes face. Players should report by at least 2:00 p.m. for taping and meetings in order to be prepared for the 3:30 practice, endure at least three hours of high-intensity workouts, shower, look at more films, and then leave the Duffy Daugherty Building around 8:00 p.m. This composite doesn't include voluntary weightlifting, which is highly recommended for linemen who wish to stay alive. So, add two hours a day, minimum. Standouts like monster lineman Tony Mandarich would often arrive at dawn and pump iron furiously until practice began. Usually, though, mornings are filled with classes—or, at least, they should be—and nights offer rest, studying, or perhaps the temptation of hitting a local watering hole. "As we all know, Michigan State University is a great place to be social," says Pat Shurmur. For a student-athlete with a schedule this full, going to class can sometimes "get in the way." According to communications professor James Donahue, it's often ignored altogether.

"Every once in a while I will have an athlete come to class half the time," he says. "If an athlete comes to class 50 percent of the time, that is above average."

Even with a mediocre attendance record, a student-athlete can still attain a degree. "I think you can do it," says former quarterback Dave Yarema, who led the Big Ten in passing in 1986. "It's tough to do, but it's not as tough as everyone makes it out to be. You just learn to get it done."

Learn to get it done. Yarema graduated in five years. While it's certainly not impossible to participate in football and earn a degree, it's nevertheless questionable whether student-athletes can honestly pursue both at an exemplary level. Professor Donahue doesn't think so.

"Each profession has a particular mind set," he says. "For a football player, it's competition, the notion that winning is number one. There is also the feeling that you can do anything you need to do to win. It's legal as long as you don't get caught. And that's the type of mind set they bring into the classroom, which has always demanded the exact opposite. That's a place for integrity, and that creates an inherent tension between priorities. They try to do anything just to pass."

That strategy, of course, leads to trouble. But a similar blind devotion toward academics can also hurt a student-athlete at a major program.

"There are risks to both approaches," explains Professor Van Tassell. "If you go toward academics, you may be in trouble if you don't perform and lose your scholarship. On the other hand, if you go to football, and you drop below the required GPA to stay here, you're in trouble, too. They really are on a tightrope here."

Not all players can toe the line because, quite simply, not everyone who wears a jersey is a star. Some aren't even close. Some never even step on the football field. When a football program has 90 scholarships to fill, and an average of only 40 players see action each game, inevitably there will be an overabundance of personnel. While a few stars receive the accolades, the preferential treatment, and the crowd's cheers, the vast majority of players are lost within the depth charts and never see the light of day—the light of Saturday.

David Kiel never thought he would be one of them. Despite an injury that marred his senior year at Chelsea High School, the six-foot-seven 280-pounder was a valued recruit in the Midwest. He felt worthy of the attention and the phone calls, but the whirlwind process began taking its toll on the 17-year-old. "You're getting phone calls all the time, and that puts a lot of pressure on a young kid," Kiel says. "I mean, they come to your games, they come to your practices. It's so built up. It takes away from your school and everything. It's like you're making the biggest decision of your life, and you have all these coaches telling you this and that. It's tough."

After a week, it came down to choosing Northwestern or Michigan State. Spartan Assistant Coach Norm Parker visited Kiel and gave him the ultimate pitch: "We want you first, but we're also looking at another kid. We need you today." A flustered Kiel didn't wait long to commit. "I didn't want to be left out," he explains.

Parker's last words were: "We're going to work hard and we want you to work hard, too." Four years of frustration followed for Kiel. The only playing time he experienced was during a two-minute interlude in a 1986 rout of Western Michigan University, and he once considered transferring to Central Michigan University. Instead, Kiel stuck it out, just as so many others did, and will. He spent two hours a day in the weight room, attended all the grueling winter running workouts at 6:30 each morning, and never missed a practice in four years.

And yet, no one knows his name.

"I always had the hope that I would play," Kiel says, who bypassed his final year of eligibility in 1988 to concentrate on academics. "I always said, 'If I'm going to prove myself, this will be the year.' There was always that glimmer of hope. That's what you're driving for. Just to play. I worked my butt off for four years just to play. I mean, it's like a job. It's seven days a week. A friend and I worked it out for all the time we put in, and it came down to 20 cents an hour. I put everything I had into that team."

He stops, perhaps not wishing to relive the humbling reality of shattered expectations. Like countless other members of George Perles' early reconstructive recruiting classes, Kiel lived the football life without actually playing football. But at least he completed his building construction management degree in June 1989 and says it was worth the sweat and pain.

But Kiel, speaking four days after being laid off from a construction job, has had trouble making the transition from hopeful recruit to forgotten soldier. There is an emptiness that Kiel may never fill. He loved football: He was an athlete. Despite a Rose Bowl ring, disappointment still lingers. Quite possibly, it may never go away.

"I wasn't the best athlete, but I tried," he says. "I tried. I always hoped I could make it and run on that field just one time. It was like I never even played. All I ever wanted to do was run out there and play the game. It was just like four years of practice and nothing else."

He swallows and does not continue. Kiel won't admit what seems to be next on his tongue: that he was used. Instead, he slips on his jacket and says good-bye. Perhaps it is better that way.

◆ ◆ ◆

There is a recurring theme throughout this chapter, and it comes down to one word: exploitation. Not every athlete will admit it, or want to admit it, but it is there, as evident around the Duffy Daugherty Football Building as the green carpet. Players are brought in and asked to strain and punish and risk their bodies for four or five years. In exchange, they receive the camaraderie of the football team, the chance to play a sport they dearly love, and the opportunity to obtain an academic degree—although they are not given adequate time to pursue this degree. While the athletic department collects as much as $18 from each of the 76,000 fans who pile into Spartan Stadium to be entertained, the entertainers on the field see none of this revenue. It is supposed to be enough for them just to be there, entertaining.

"What's the purpose of the football program? It's to make money for the athletic department. Not for the academic portion of the university or for the athletes themselves. The whole system is out of control," says Professor Donahue. "What if I went before the trustees with a proposal for my own program, where I bring in these kids, many of whom are disadvantaged minorities, make them work real hard, hardly give them a chance to go to school, but let the university make a lot of money from them? Do you think they would let me do that? Heck, no. I'd get fired on the spot. And yet, that's essentially what the football program is doing.

"My heart goes out to all those minority student-athletes who are brought in here. They are the most abused because they are the most vulnerable."

Vulnerable perhaps, but not dumb. Cornerback Derrick Reed transferred to Michigan State from scandal-ridden Southern Methodist University in 1987. He experienced two major-college programs, one that was drowning in illegalities and the other that was deemed relatively clean by NCAA standards. But the bottom line of both programs is the same: exploitation.

"You realize a lot of stuff when you graduate," says Reed, now a sales representative with Moore Business Forms in Dallas. "People don't realize a lot of the pressure, the hard work, and dedication that a college athlete has to go through. People have to realize that. Everybody thinks it's all fun and games, but I see it now. I'm in the business world, and I can finally relate to it. The college athlete is used. When I say used, I mean they don't get what they deserve. Fine, they get a scholarship. That's fine. They get a free education, but it should be more than that. The university should help them get jobs after they graduate. We're going to get some connections because we're known, but there should be more done. They should realize that. I really feel sometimes they should get more than just academics out of it."

That is a point sometimes overlooked. The majority of student-athletes are not the monosyllabic, dumb jocks shamelessly portrayed on HBO comedy specials. They are intelligent young people who read newspapers. When stories appear in these papers about the Big Ten receiving $6 million from the Rose Bowl, or about the next multi-million-dollar television contract signed by a conference, these young people—especially those who saw parents struggle for every dollar and cent—begin to wonder what has happened to their portion of the pie. Then the realization hits: They are still considered amateur players and have no claim to the profits. Add to this the fact that the NCAA prohibits athletes from working during the regular school year, and these young people become, in effect, economic prisoners on campus. These entertainers must be content with empty wallets.

"How could you not feel you shouldn't get some payments, or something out of the deal?" asks Reed, who graduated from Michigan State with a marketing management degree in 1989, shortly after his senior season. "You can't work, so how are you supposed to get money? You can't receive any sort of payments. Basically, you get your scholarship and have to depend on your parents and other guys. Not everyone has the type of background where you have money sent to you every week. A lot of guys walk around without any money in their pockets, and I just think the system needs to be changed. Let them work, or something, because it's bad. It's bad. There've been many days that I've walked the streets without any money. It's not fair."

Sadly, few athletes, if any, realize what they are missing out on while they are in uniform. They put faith in the coach and in all his platitudes—such as "Hard work builds character and discipline"—that fill each practice session. These idealistic motivational tools do not fall apart while football is still around. That generally occurs later, along with the realization that their talents were prostituted for the economic benefit of no one but the athletic department.

"You're used, no doubt about it," says Craig Johnson. "You're used while you're there and while you can play. After that, hey, you're on your own. You're definitely being used. I don't think any player can say they weren't while they were there."

Michigan State University isn't an ugly aberration in an otherwise pristine world of college athletics. Offenses such as these occur at nearly every college program—and other schools run to the bank right alongside Michigan State. However, this doesn't make the situation any easier to accept.

Soothing talk of academic priorities flows easily from Perles' mouth, yet a hard look at the facts does not back up his claims. Perhaps it is unfair to hold him solely accountable for the numbers; realistically, not every recruit has the classroom foremost on his mind. But many do, and, as evidenced in this chapter, those educational aspirations can easily be dwarfed by the pressures of football. Wherever the blame lies, the following figures are both important and disturbing.

Of Perles' 1983 and 1984 recruiting classes—the only two groups of recruits that have had enough time to be accurately gauged—28 of 58 players recruited (48 percent) had graduated by winter term 1990. In that same time period, 25 of the 40 players (62 percent) who lettered in football earned a degree. Finally, 25 of the 31 of these players who completed their eligibility (80 percent) graduated. The numbers, obtained through Michigan State University's registrar's office and graduation records, shatter two previously accepted truths: 1) that the football program's graduation rate is higher than that of the general student body; and 2) that George Perles graduates "everyone who completes his eligibility," which he often claims.

Cherryl Jensen, director of MSU's news bureau, reports that 60 percent of the university's incoming student body from 1983 to 1984 had graduated by the fall term of 1989. By contrast, just 15 of 33 recruits (43 percent) in Perles' initial 1983 recruiting class and 13 of 25 recruits (52 percent) from the 1984 class had graduated at that time. It is important to remember that graduation rates are usually higher for football recruits than for the overall student body, because athletes have significant incentive—namely, a full-ride scholarship— to stay in school. Yet, George Perles' first two classes have not been the academic successes they are commonly thought to be.

Charlie Wilson, MSU's assistant athletic director in charge of academic counseling, has called Perles' 1983 recruiting class "one of the best academic classes in the history of Michigan State." That certainly sounds impressive, until one looks more closely and begins, then, to worry about the other, less successful recruiting classes.

What of the starters, the athletes we see on the field and whose personalities and talents we have come to admire? Of the 19 junior and senior starters on the 1987 Rose Bowl team, 11(58 percent) had graduated by spring term 1990—allowing them at least six years to complete a degree. To obtain a little historical perspective, the following question should be posed: Did that conference title come at the expense of academic performance? Probably. Compare that percentage to a team from the less-than-inspiring Muddy Waters era, the 3-8 squad in 1981. That team graduated 16 of 22 starters (73 percent). Granted, the 1981 players have had considerably more time to achieve a degree, but the prospect of the Rose Bowl team's percentage increasing dramatically is minimal, according to Beth Shapiro, deputy director of the Michigan State University library. Her 1982 study of 25 years of Spartan athletics (1950 to 1974) found nine out of ten athletes who earn a degree do so within six years. The remaining ten percent rarely graduate after this six-year mark. "After that period, you always have one or two who will finish maybe ten years after they started, but that's rare," says Shapiro. "Usually six years is enough time to get a general picture."

So, how do the academic records of Perles' teams stack up against the cumulative effort of his predecessors, Biggie Munn, Duffy Daugherty, and Denny Stolz? Thus far, Perles is lagging a bit behind. Shapiro's study says that from 1950 to 1974, 67 percent of all football recruits graduated. Perles' number: 48 percent. Also, of those players from 1950 to 1974 who had earned a letter in football, 81 percent also earned a degree. Perles' mark with letter-winners: 62 percent.

Again, the time element involved may be a factor in Perles' lower figures, but Shapiro says it is a small one.

She also feels the type of student-athlete coming to Michigan State University and to other major-college programs plays a role.

"I think a whole lot of athletes are coming in here thinking they are the next Magic Johnson or Kirk Gibson, and it's a great shock to them when they aren't," says Shapiro, who researched "Intercollegiate Athletics and Big-Time Sport at MSU" for her master's degree in philosophy. "If they don't realize this very early, then they get run over roughshod and they come out without anything. The kids before were coming here to get an education. But now all that has changed. Football is their ticket for fame and fortune, and getting an education is secondary. Television gave prominence to the games. Now they're going to college for a way into the pros instead of football giving them a way into college."

There is one area where George Perles' record is in line with the past: minority student-athletes at Michigan State. Shapiro's study reports that 55.4 percent of minority recruits from 1950 to 1974 have graduated. Excluding junior-college transfer students, 13 minority recruits from Perles' initial two classes have earned a letter playing football. Six (46 percent) had graduated by winter term 1990. It may be too early to draw any firm conclusions from such a small base of minority letter-winners. Nevertheless, the statistic bothers professors such as history professor Harry Reed, who is black.

"It disturbs me for a number of reasons," begins Reed. "These kids keep getting lulled into the meat grinder, and there seem to be few ways to hold Perles' toe to the fire to make him interested in his kids getting an education or graduating. They have a tutorial system in place, but kids can go or not go. There hardly seems to be a significant kind of follow-up. It ought to be possible to give these kids at least a minimal education. It's just a vicious game."

More often than not, it is the student-athlete who loses at this game. "It seems to me that as a group—and obviously there are some exceptions—but, as a group, this is an exploited class of student," remarks history professor Levine. "It's indefensible for a football coach to try to arrange for one of his athletes to take final exams while he's in jail. It's pathetic. It underlines the way the system exploits kids."

The man paid $22,380 annually to perform the seedier portions of this exploitation is 36-year-old Greg Croxton, Michigan State University's student advisor for athletic student affairs, who played under Denny Stoltz as a Spartan offensive lineman from 1973 to 1975. A native of Highland Park, Michigan, Croxton graduated with a bachelor's degree in urban studies in 1976 and earned a master's degree in 1987.

Croxton, who is black, sometimes acts as a buffer between the explosive Perles and the black players in the football program. "He's valuable as an assistant coach because he has the job of implementing hands-on the discipline that George lays out," says Pat Shurmur, who worked closely with both men as a graduate assistant in 1988. "If George has to discipline a black player, it might not be well taken. They might think the world is out to get them. I mean, I like to see a friendly face. I like to see somebody who's the same as me. As with running backs coach Charlie Baggett, who is also black, some of these kids like to see people who are similar to them."

But, as with the Ezor case, Croxton spends much of his time trying to keep players eligible. Mike Staisil, a former MSU lineman, said Croxton's advising duties didn't extend beyond that primary objective.

"He would make sure the borderline student-athletes would go to class and get their grades," explains Staisil. "There wasn't really any career advice, however. Nothing dealing with life after football. There should be someone to talk to them when they come in here, someone who asks them what they want to do. I mean, one injury and their careers are done. Then what?"

That is a question asked often by educators, but rarely mentioned in the endless pursuit of a football dynasty, where the highest academic priority is to keep players eligible. This is the area in which Croxton operates—and it is a job that quite frequently upsets professors.

"Greg Croxton's specialty is badgering professors," James Donahue remarks from his communications department office. "He's widely known around the university for that. Basically, his job is to get grades for students who don't go to class. I don't know how most of them stay eligible. I've gotten calls from him lots of times. There are two types of calls. In the first scenario, if a student from another department is clearly going to fail, Croxton will call here begging for me to allow the student an independent study. This is two or three weeks before the term ends. The second type of call occurs when a student has hardly shown up for class and I flunk him. Croxton will call two or three days later and say, 'Can't you do something for this guy?'"

Greg Croxton has been contacted for interviews in the past, but he has refused to talk unless the reporter first cleared it with George Perles. What an indication of where this man stands—directly under Perles' thumb (indeed, his office is less than 50 feet from the head coach's). But, in a way, Croxton stands in front of Perles, shielding him, stubbornly willing to accept any bullets that may be forthcoming. He prudently remains silent unless Perles gives him the OK, but any embarrassing academic situations never reach the top. They fall conveniently on Croxton's husky shoulders. That, plain and simple, is his job.

Many think it's a job that rarely has the athlete's best interest in mind. "I think we do our athletes a disservice," says Professor Harry Reed, who has watched vulnerable athletes be shuttled through the system for 20 years. "We either have to make the term 'student-athlete' mean something and hold them to the same academic standards that we hold the rest of the student body to, or we should simply understand that they are here for entertainment purposes only, and pay them. The administration is being dishonest in the way it treats athletes."

Indeed, when honesty does seep into conversations, the answers are troubling. When asked in 1988 why Northwestern's football team is often inept compared to Michigan State's, Croxton offered this simple explanation: "There ain't no books on the 50-yard line."

◆ ◆ ◆

Meanwhile, Blake Ezor will probably go without a degree. He signed up for a communications class for the winter term of 1990, drawing media raves about his taking education seriously. However, according to teaching assistant Jenny Grau, he didn't attend class once; preparing for the National Football League draft took precedence. Football, as before, came first.

"It probably could have been handled better," says Ezor, "but it was done last-minute. If I don't graduate out of here [spring term], then I'm going to say it was a bad decision."

As it turned out, Ezor didn't graduate in June of 1990; instead, he was arrested for a price tag switch at a local supermarket. He was charged on June 25 for misrepresenting merchandise, a misdemeanor that could carry a jail sentence of up to 90 days. Maybe now he's ready to say that missing finals week was a bad decision. But since Ezor's four years as a Spartan athlete are over, he might be the only one to openly admit this. Because there will be more swift tailbacks who fearlessly drive into the enemy's ranks. There will be more 1,000-yard seasons, more deafening cheers, more fall classics.

And there will be more lies.

"George Perles is the biggest hypocrite on the face of the earth," concludes Professor Donahue. "His hypocrisy is mind-boggling. He has no interest in these kids as students at all."

3

THE STEROID QUESTION

"I wasn't going in the ring to box with Mike Tyson. I was going in there to kick his ass."

> – Tony Mandarich, March 1, 1990

Rumors of steroid use have haunted the Spartan football program for several years, prompting subtle and sometimes not-so-subtle questions from reporters who, treading on unfamiliar ground, were not always sure just what to ask. Pat Shurmur told us of a "doctor's team" made up of players who tested positive for steroids and other drugs during probable cause testing within the program. Shurmur also said he believed Tony Mandarich had used steroids, and that the drug created a division between those MSU linemen who "juiced" and those who didn't. In addition, former linebacker Tim Moore admitted to using steroids soon after the 1987 season to prepare himself for the NFL combines.

But these testimonies paled in comparison to the knowledge that former walk-on Spartan Jeff Case shared with the Detroit *News* and became headlines on March 21, 1990. Case told the *News:* 1) Michigan State players supplied one another with steroids and syringes and injected each other with the drug; 2) they falsified NCAA drug tests by using "urine bags" taped to their bodies to supply clean samples; and 3) Mandarich was looked upon as the steroid "mentor," supplying and injecting team-mates at his off-campus apartment. Although these allega-tions have yet to be proven, Michigan State University has not produced one bit of information to dispute the claims of rampant steroid use among members of its football program.

Mandarich refused to be interviewed for the Detroit *News* article, but he agreed to sit down and discuss his turbulent life for the benefit of this book, just three weeks before Case's damaging testimony became public knowledge. What follows is his story, with additional insight provided by Tim Moore; Pat Shurmur; Mandarich's bodybuilding advisor, Rory Leidelmeyer; and several steroid experts.

◆ ◆ ◆

If a man talks big, and appears big, do we automatically assume that he feels big? That depends on how you feel about the "savage tan" that Tony Mandarich is sporting in East Lansing on a brisk March afternoon. Is this the result of a jet-setting junket in Cancun, or three hours in a large tanning booth? With a grinning Mandarich enjoying the confusion created by the tan, it is up to the beholder to attempt to separate fact from fantasy.

Just what is artificial and what is real about Mandarich has been a popular topic of debate ever since he became a legitimate superstar on Michigan State's offensive line in 1987. His Canadian heritage, his fondness for heavy metal music, and his six-foot-six, 315-pound frame make him an intriguing character; his loud mouth and alleged ties to anabolic steroids make him a rebel. In fact, others have spent so much time and energy trying to figure out who Tony Mandarich is that he has begun to wonder himself.

After quitting school, moving to Los Angeles, and being drafted second overall by the Green Bay Packers, Mandarich signed late and suffered through a humiliating rookie season in 1989—one with little playing time and even less satisfaction. He returned to East Lansing, signed up for a winter term class, and barely attended. He also acquired the tan. But by his own admission, he only talks a good game now, resulting more from learning about real life than from learning about humility. Mandarich is not humbled, but he doesn't feel nearly as big as he did when experts declared him the greatest offensive lineman of all time.

"Once I get back to the level I was at, where I can crush and manhandle people again, then I'll go back to saying what I feel," he says in the relaxed emptiness of the Powerhouse Gym, his lifting haven in East Lansing. A giant portrait of Mandarich adorns an outside wall, and he is indeed a hero inside. A hero by accident? Not quite. Despite the relative timidity that emanates from Mandarich these days, he worked long and hard to cultivate an image that still exists: the image of Terrible Tony.

"People will say I give better interviews than other athletes, but it's just that I'm not afraid to say what I feel," Manadrich says. "I've always believed in saying what I feel, but in some other people's eyes that will come out in an arrogant way. It's not that other athletes aren't being honest; it's just that they're saying things that won't turn people's heads. They're blending in."

Which is something Mandarich can never be accused of. Ever since he moved from his hometown of Oakville, Ontario to stay with his brother, John, in an apartment near Kent State University in 1983, he has found ways of standing apart from the crowd. While John was playing for Kent State, Tony enrolled at Kent Roosevelt High School so he could easily obtain a scholarship from an American university. Mandarich is imbued with an intoxicating appreciation for money, and he figured America—and the NFL, in particular—was where the big money would be available.

"The whole thing was a plan, and it was a long shot, because less than one percent of all people who throw on a helmet make it to the pro level," says Mandarich. "But the plan was to make it."

Before he could "make it"—make headlines, make money, make history—Mandarich had to make himself conspicuous. Just 235 pounds when signed on to play in East Lansing, he weighed well over 270 pounds by 1986 at the beginning of his sophomore season. He changed the spelling of his last name (from Mandaric) because people had mispronounced it too often.

"Personally, I think everything that happened to him was planned," says former Spartan quarterback Dave Yarema. "If you're in the pros, any publicity is good, whether it's good or bad. But I liked him. He was full of energy all the time. He was heavy metal. He always wore this leather jacket. He was Mr. Heavy Metal, hanging out at [East Lansing's] Silver Dollar Saloon."

It was in the spring of 1986 that George Perles started thinking that someone so big and yet so quick should be inflicting pain on quarterbacks. Mandarich played defensive end in that season's spring game and was named defensive player of the game. After taunting and shoving Yarema, a senior, to the point of malice, Mandarich stood in the locker room after the game, expounding on his love for this new and exciting position. "I'm kind of glad I made the move," he said euphorically. "It's kind of fun." Then, inexplicably, Perles moved him back to the offensive line. Injuries there had taken their toll, and Mandarich would

never play defense again—which made more than one Big
Ten quarterback think that there was a God after all, and
all was indeed right with the world.

By the time the 1987 Rose Bowl season rolled around,
Mandarich's size had become the subject of national
conversation. He weighed more than 300 pounds, which
he claimed was the result of furious workouts at the
Powerhouse Gym. "The only way you can get publicity on
the offensive line is if you're one of the elite," he said before
the season began. "It's there for the asking; I've just got to
grab it. During the off-season, I'm in the weight room at
least six, sometimes seven days a week. On most teams,
I think, the leader is determined by seniority. Here, we do
it by who works hardest."

Mandarich played more minutes than any other Spartan during that historic season, earning All-American
honors en route to a Big Ten championship and the victory
in Pasadena. He was named the Big Ten Offensive
Lineman of the Year. Perles called him "the best offensive
lineman I've ever been associated with."

Mr. Heavy Metal was lifting just that, bench-pressing
475 pounds and squatting 630. He ran a 4.69 40-yard
dash, which was incredibly fast for someone his size. In
short, he was absolutely on fire—and he knew it. "I think
I realized I could really do it after the Rose Bowl year," he
says of his NFL aspirations. "I started putting pressure on
myself and thinking my back was against the wall. I knew
if I worked hard in the winter and spring and played well
in the fall, I'd get drafted."

Patience has never been one of Mandarich's attributes.
His familiarity with the concept has never extended much
beyond the lyrics crooned by his hero, Axl Rose of the
heavy metal band Guns 'n Roses. So in January 1988,
right after the Rose Bowl victory, when his brother John
suggested that Tony, now 319 pounds, declare hardship

and apply for the NFL draft, it became a matter of intense consideration.

"I hadn't had enough of Michigan State; I'd had enough of college," says Mandarich, a communications major who was still 24 credits shy of a degree in the spring of 1990. "I just wanted to move on, because they were already saying I was the best offensive lineman in history. If they were saying that, then I thought my chances were pretty good. So we got really serious about it after the [April 1988] draft had already been held. That's why we wrote a letter for the supplemental draft."

The fateful letter entered the mail two weeks after the draft and caused instant trouble for both Mandarich and Michigan State University as soon as the news media and the NCAA caught wind of it.

Suddenly, Mandarich was perceived as a greedy and sadistic lunatic from Canada who was spitting in the face of America's scholastic values. He was both obnoxious and obstinate, the nation was told by columnists playing a hunch. He was ambitious. He was a stomach-turning example of how lust for money was corrupting all that was pure and good in modern society. And Tony Mandarich was loving every minute of it.

"The positive that came out of the whole thing was that I got a lot of publicity," says Mandarich, who believes the episode may have raised his pro stock. "People got to know who Tony Mandarich was, whether they liked him or didn't like him. I was always a renegade and a rebel, but the reason I wasn't a rebel on the national level was because I wasn't getting the national publicity."

Perles didn't find out about the letter until May 24, more than a month after it had been submitted. He immediately began telling reporters that it was a letter of inquiry, not an application, though Mandarich now says such an assertion was false. One reporter who wrote about the letter as an application was verbally assaulted by Perles, who believed such articles hurt Michigan State's chances to get its star lineman back on campus for the fall season.

"He knows I want him to stay," said Perles. "For selfish reasons and because I believe it's best for him."

Mandarich says he withdrew the request two days before the supplemental draft because he hadn't heard from the NFL one way or the other. He feared not being able to play football at all in 1988. The NCAA, through Michigan State, still suspended him for the season—a penalty that was later reduced to three games.

"I still say what the NCAA did was wrong," Mandarich asserts. "I can see what they meant by the mistake, but they could have just given me a one-game suspension. Some say they could have given me a full-year suspension, but if they had done that I would have played pro that year. There are so many ways to think about it."

Mandarich was particularly repulsed by an August 24 conference call with the NCAA that ultimately decided his fate. It involved Perles, MSU Athletic Director Doug Weaver, faculty representative Mike Kasavana, Mandarich, and three members of the NCAA's eligibility committee. "I thought if I faxed them something that said, 'Look, I'm withdrawing from the draft, I want no part of it,' then they'd say everything was cool and done. But they had to have their little meeting, which I thought was very amateurish. It was like six kids on the block arguing over whether or not I could play soccer with them."

The Spartans, who wore Mandarich's number 79 on their helmets for the first three games, lost to Rutgers, Notre Dame, and Florida State without their leader, and needed to win their last six games to gain a Gator Bowl berth. Mandarich himself was stigmatized in the press because of his brush with NCAA sanctions and because of his perceived repudiation of MSU in favor of an early shot at the NFL. Rumors of steroid use had been debated in the papers for several years, and his belligerent attitude had helped fan those flames of speculation. Eventually, the flames rose high enough for Mandarich to feel the heat.

"I wouldn't recommend [steroids], but to each his own," he wrote in a guest column for the Lansing *State Journal* on May 9, 1988. "There's no doubt steroids can hurt you physically. And they can hurt you in the newspaper, the way they did Timmy Moore."

◆ ◆ ◆

Tim Moore remembers the phone ringing at about two in the morning. He was sleeping soundly after a hard workout with the Phoenix Cardinals, an NFL team he was trying out for after his eligibility had been used up at Michigan State in 1987.

It was a reporter from the Phoenix *Gazette*, saying he had drug testing reports from the NFL combines in front of him. He said he knew Moore had tested positive for steroids.

"I said, 'So, what do you want?'" Moore explains. "He said, 'What do you have to say about it?'"

What could Moore say? An All-American linebacker noted for his ferocity at Michigan State from 1984 to 1987, Moore realized he wasn't big enough to make it in the NFL. He had used steroids at Michigan State with success, according to Jeff Case. So, after the Spartans won the Rose Bowl and Moore participated in two senior all-star games, the Japan Bowl and the Senior Bowl, he wasn't fearful when he obtained the illegal drug and did a "cycle" three weeks before reporting to the combines.

"I was 210 pounds and I had to go to the combines," says Moore, who now says the Phoenix reporter lied about having the testing reports. "The pros aren't even going to look at a linebacker who's 210. So I got on them and I was on them for three or four weeks. I knew I was going to test positive, but I didn't care. I just wanted to get bigger, you know. I thought they'd look at steroids as something I was using to try to enhance myself."

The Cardinals didn't. They cut Moore early. In 1989, he tried out for the Green Bay Packers, mainly because former Spartan player and coach Hank Bullough was defensive coordinator. Perles and Bullough are extremely close, and Perles led Moore to believe that Green Bay offered an inside shot.

"I thought Hank Bullough was a tough coach who liked tough players," says Moore, who made the developmental squad but was cut after four weeks. "That's not how it is. That's not what he likes. He's the one who canned me, let's put it that way. He personally was the one who cut me. [Head Coach] Lindy Infante told me, 'We sat in a meeting all last night talking about who should be cut, and Hank Bullough came up with you.'"

Now Moore is using Mandarich's agent, Cleveland-based Vern Sharbaugh, because he doesn't feel Perles has done enough to further his career. "He never liked agents, and I always listened to him," says Moore. "But he hasn't done shit for me. He's too busy now. He doesn't have time for me."

The publicity surrounding Moore's admission to using steroids could have contributed to his failure to crack an NFL roster. He conceded that possibility as he sipped a beer and gazed about the interior of Dooley's, an East Lansing bar that was his favorite stomping ground when he was an MSU player. It's empty now on a February afternoon. Moore, who was stuffing grocery bags at a supermarket one year after his heroic Rose Bowl performance, has yet to graduate. He's working in a Lansing Coca-Cola warehouse and is still seeking a bachelor's degree in criminal justice. He has been a student at Michigan State for more than seven years.

"Football took up all of my time," says Moore, who is third on the Spartan all-time tackles list with 332. "I would screw around and all of my effort and time went into football. I wanted to play pro ball and that was my only goal in life. When I got cut, that was a little bit of an eye-opener."

Moore still refuses to relinquish this impossible dream. He still believes that a bigger Tim Moore could be a success in pro football. For now, however, he is starting that trek at the bottom: the Bath Cardinals of the Michigan Amateur Football League.

"I've always been a lot smaller than everyone else," says the 218-pound Moore. "I've just always thought I had to go out and kick everybody's ass. I haven't done steroids since—that's why I'm so light. I used to hang out at all the gyms in Lansing. Steroids are all over. Everybody's saying, 'Get huge. Get huge.'"

Todd Elsea, a teammate of Moore's at St. John's High School and now his roommate and trainer, concurs. "He could do them right now if he wanted to," he says of Moore and steroids. "I could get them for him in an hour."

Probably faster. It is difficult for anyone who has been in or around major-college football to ignore the presence of these performance-enhancing drugs. The drive to make an NFL roster that turned Moore to steroids is also present in the minds of other college athletes. David Kiel, a six-foot-seven, 280-pound lineman, suffered through four long seasons of not being good enough. He entered just one game. An illegal substance that offered an edge was clearly an option, and he admitted the idea entered his mind. "I thought about it a couple times," explains Kiel, who said he resisted the temptation to use steroids. "There's a lot of competition and pressure for the athlete to perform. The desire just to get into a game might be enough for some guys to do it, to go to that extreme. I mean, you're there to play football and you're working so hard just to get out on the field, that you think about it.

You would see people with added strength and size, and that's how they did it."

♦ ♦ ♦

The Spartans' quarter-million-dollar weight and conditioning facility provides ample opportunity to add bulk. It's become a shrine to Strength and Conditioning Coach David Henry and his pupils, who spend a large amount of their day pumping iron. The screeches of heavy metal music drown out the clanking and exhausting groans that fill this portion of the Duffy Daugherty Football Building.

It is the showplace of the Perles era. The composite Spartan lineman in 1988 weighed 277 pounds—42 pounds heavier than the average Michigan State up-front man at the beginning of the decade. That added muscle has produced the most consistent rushing attack in the Big Ten—and has also sparked questions about unnatural practices. Still, the weight room is a source of great pride for the team.

"There are kids who spend 10 to 12 hours a day here," said Henry in a 1988 interview. "Everybody does their share, because everyone is going after the same thing. It's a combination of the athletes, the staff, and the facilities. It all fuels itself. The intensity, toughness, regimentation, discipline, and whatever it takes. That's why they spend morning 'til night here. What goes around comes around. It's kind of like a cycle."

But are hard work and determination the only ingredients in producing bigger and better linemen? Not always.

The shroud of secrecy regarding Michigan State and steroids cannot be overemphasized. There is fear—great fear—that physical retribution will meet anyone who leaks the steroid secret. That is why only two players used their names in the Detroit *News* story. Not surprisingly, both of those men were no longer on the team. There are times, of course, when alcohol loosens lips and players will unknowingly boast about the effectiveness of the drug to other bar patrons, who just happen to be reporters. But that testimony can never be repeated the next morning sober. The risk, they feel, is too great.

Take, for instance, the story of one Michigan State senior. As a member of the powerlifting team, he regularly works out at the Duffy Daugherty Football Building. He has heard steroids openly discussed by football players in the weight room. He confirms that steroids are there. But he declined to elaborate further. "I wish I could talk about it, but I can't. All I can say is that something needs to be done because there is a problem."

That problem, according to the Detroit *News* article, was as much a part of the Spartans' Rose Bowl season as their stifling Stunt 4-3 defense. As indicated earlier, that copyrighted March 21, 1990 story sent shock waves through the Michigan State community and affirmed a suspicion that had lingered for years: The Spartans were "juicers."

Former MSU players Jeff Case and Lance Hostetler—along with more than 100 other players, physicians, coaches, and parents—were interviewed during a two-month investigation conducted by the Detroit *News,* and some of the findings were truly grisly. While the rumored urine bag switch, mentioned in the article, had been a speculation often voiced to explain the Spartans' flawless testing mark at bowl games, the truly shocking aspect of the *News* story was the brashness and openness with which MSU players discussed having used steroids.

According to witnesses, Tony Mandarich was the primary source of information concerning steroid use, even injecting several teammates. He supposedly kept vials of drugs—including masking agents, drugs to increase aggression, and substances used to battle side effects of steroids—in a kitchen cabinet in his apartment.

When inquisitive players wondered how they could make themselves bigger, they would be directed to Mandarich's locker. There, the players would learn how to bulk up like Outland Trophy candidates. "I said, 'Tony, I want to get bigger—how do I do that?'" Jeff Case recalled in the *News* story. "He explained all about Anadrol and testosterone and how to use them in cycles . . . . He wrote out weight and diet programs for me."

Case wasn't alone. Lance Hostetler, a former offensive lineman at MSU who transferred to Kent State University, claims he purchased ten cubic centimeters of testosterone cypionate from a teammate in the Spartan locker room. He hoped a heavier frame would help him live up to coaches' expectations that "bigger was better." As Hostetler told the *News*, "The way they were talking, I was way too small."

Along with Mandarich, offensive lineman David Houle and defensive lineman John Budde were named as the team's primary steroid users. It was Houle, according to several sources, who tested positive for steroids after the 1987 season and who feared another positive result would jeopardize his status at the Rose Bowl. To insure a clean test, Houle reportedly borrowed a friend's urine sample, concealing it in a plastic bag held under his armpit with a hose running from the bag to his pants.

It has been alleged that four to seven MSU players used this urine bag trick to fool NCAA testers just prior to the 1987 Rose Bowl game. In the *News* article, Frank Uryask, the NCAA's director of testing, stated it was "unlikely" that MSU players had perpetrated the urine bag scam, and cautioned that this type of situation was "one word against another."

However it was accomplished, not one Spartan player tested positive at the 1988 Rose Bowl.

Perhaps it was this false and extremely naïve sense of purity which prompted MSU's puzzling vote at the NCAA's national convention in January 1990. Only five schools in the nation voted *against* aspects of a new mandatory random drug-testing program. Michigan State University was one.

This troubling cloud hovering over MSU did not appear overnight. Tales of unnatural practices and extraordinary performances in the school's weight room had been circulating since 1985—three years after Perles brought his pro-football mentality and size requirements to East Lansing. He told the fans to be patient, while lamenting about his lack of "fifth-year linemen." The message from the outset was clear: No 198-pound linemen were going to send Michigan State to the Rose Bowl. The kids needed to be bigger.

Obviously, a shift in recruiting philosophy played some role in the surreal weight gains and subsequent dominant rushing attack. Perles' recruiting efforts concentrated on two primary areas: running backs and bulky offensive linemen who could bludgeon Big Ten defenses, opening holes for the highly touted MSU tailbacks. More than one recruiting day during the formative years of the Perles era saw offensive coach Buck Nystrom (1983 to 1986) remark with wonderment, "These kids we're bringing in keep getting bigger."

And stronger. By the 1985 season, the Spartan weight room boasted 21 players who could bench press more than 400 pounds—a mark few other schools could match. Since that time, the number has never dipped below a dozen; some players have even penetrated the 500-pound per lift plateau. All this grunt and gain, quite naturally, became the trademark for a team searching for national respectability. "When I came here, I was intimidated by everyone's size," Dave Houle said. "Me, [defensive lineman Mark] Nichols, and the whole group wanted to get as strong as we could be."

That desire apparently turned some players toward using steroids to attain the goal. Nancy Spencer, who tutors MSU athletes, recalls instances in which football players were quite open about their affection for steroids. Several, she told the Detroit *News*, even brought syringes to her tutoring sessions.

But concerns about possible drug abuse waned under the giddiness of MSU's breakthrough year and the possibility of the school's first Heisman Trophy winner, Lorenzo White. They were dubbed "The White Knights," these oversized offensive linemen of 1986. Mandarich, a red-shirt sophomore, was still relatively small at 267 pounds, but senior Doug Rogers weighed in at 280, while Dave Houle, a junior, had grown to 270 pounds.

Houle was a curious case. The 6-foot-4 lineman from Plymouth, Michigan came to MSU lighter than quarterback Dave Yarema, who weighed 213 pounds. But in successive years, Houle's weight jumped from 205 to 220, 245, 270, and, finally, to 280 in 1987. Nichols, Houle's roommate, had ballooned from 228 to 255 pounds during the 1986 off-season, and he had increased his bench strength capabilities from 335 pounds to a remarkable 500 pounds. "I knew I had to get bigger to get better," Nichols explained.

Of course, there was also Mandarich, who was only beginning to sculpt his legend. Leading into his junior year, he would add another 30 pounds of bulk. For his collegiate finale, Mandarich jumped to 319 pounds of pure athlete—some trainers claimed he actually topped 330 when that season began. Journalists and opposing coaches alike began wondering how Mandarich could beef up so quickly without losing a trace of speed. Later, in the afterglow of the Rose Bowl triumph, the whispers—damaging allegations that the Spartans were a steroid-ridden squad—heightened. The whispers have never been silenced.

Michigan State University is not the only school field-
ing a roster tainted by talk of steroid abuse. There are
estimates from former NCAA players that 50 percent of
Big Ten linemen have used these drugs. In a 1985 study
conducted at Michigan State, Dr. Douglas McKeag and Dr.
William Anderson surveyed 2,000 college athletes and
found that 5 percent were using steroids. "However, it's
10 percent in football," says Frank Uryasz, NCAA director
of testing. "And one out of ten college players using
steroids is a problem." So is the fact that 6.6 percent of
high school males have experimented with the drug. A
1988 survey of more than 3,400 high school males conducted by the Penn State Department of Health and
Human Development reported that nearly half of those
testing positive had used steroids for improved athletic
performance. Steroids have, sadly, become a part of the
game.

But at what cost? While the long-range dangers associated with steroid abuse have yet to be fully understood
and documented, several serious side effects of anabolic
steroids are well known. Among them are:

- The shrinking of the testes and possible sterility in
  males.
- A phenomenon described as "roid rage"— aggressive behavior underlined by dramatic mood swings
  and outbursts of violence.
- Life-threatening danger to the liver.
- Cardiovascular damage, which can trigger strokes,
  heart attacks, and a plaque buildup in the arteries.
- Acne, yellowing of skin, hair loss.

Too often, however, these medical risks never enter an
athlete's mind. "It is clear that athletes will engage in
extreme behaviors if they believe they can gain a 'winning
edge,'" writes Dr. David Lamb of Purdue University's
Department of Physical Education, Health, and Recrea-
tional Studies. "Some of the athletes, who stand on the

verge of fame and fortune if they can obtain an advantage
using anabolic drugs, care little that such drugs are illegal
or harmful."

Consider the story of Nebraska All-Amerian Dean
Steinkuhler, who in 1986 admitted he used steroids while
playing for the Cornhuskers and in the pros. The drug
immediately resulted in a 15-pound increase (from 260
to 275 pounds) and a 50-pound jump in his bench presses
(to 350 pounds). "I wanted to be the best I could be," he
told *Sports Illustrated.* "I wanted to be better than anyone
else. I thought I was a good athlete, but I needed something
to get me over the hump."

That is a line repeated by many athletes who have
dabbled with steroids. According to *The Physician and
Sportsmedicine,* steroids are most effective when the
athlete has reached a plateau in training—when increases
no longer bring results. So steroids effectively open the
next door.

"There comes a point . . . when height and weight begin
to limit performance and narrow the opportunity in
sports," writes Dr. William Taylor in his book, *Hormonal
Manipulation: A New Era of Monstrous Athletes.* "Those
of us who work with athletes know a few added inches or
pounds could mean the difference between standout or
mediocrity, fortune or a life on the production line.

"Peer pressure is a strong motivator," he continues,
"especially if young athletes see themselves being out-
stripped by the competition. It could be a case of 'either
take the drugs or don't play—you're not good enough.'"

This pressure to get bigger is evident after attending
just a few practices inside the Duffy Daugherty Football
Building. That is the first command young linemen hear,
and most are well aware that if they don't make the
necessary weight gains, someone will replace them—perhaps someone with a steroid advantage. So the vicious
cycle continues.

"I knew if I could just gain 20 pounds, I would play," a Spartan who admitted to using steroids told the Detroit *News.* "There's just so much pressure up here . . . all that pressure really gets to a lot of people."

An important question, then, revolves around whether George Perles and his staff can be held responsible for the time bombs ticking inside MSU players. "I'm a football coach—I don't play trainer; I don't play doctor," Perles said in a prepared response to the steroid controversy. "I want to assure everyone that the notion of winning any football game isn't even on the same page or even in the same book as our obligation to the health, care, and education of those student-athletes entrusted in our care."

Is it that easy? Aren't coaches who encourage young athletes to feverishly pump iron—and get bigger—also planting a potentially tragic seed, subliminally urging players to achieve this goal in any way possible? Experts studying situations like this believe the answer is yes.

"People who think winning is all-important subtly encourage steroid use without meaning to by telling them [student-athletes] that if they were a little bit bigger, faster, or stronger, they could start this year on the football team," says Dick Stickle, executive director of a drug education program within the National Federation of State High School Associations. Even though they would never provide athletes information on steroids—"that would be political suicide," says Dr. Douglas McKeag—coaches still can subtly influence players to take the 'steroid step.'

Michigan State University conducted just 41 steroid tests during the past four years—a time when rumors, Herculean weight room feats, and warning signals were popping up all around the Duffy Daugherty Football Building. Why wasn't Mandarich, the primary focus of the steroid question at MSU, ever tested by the school under its probable cause guidelines? Hadn't his gargantuan growth, yellow skin, receding hairline, worsening acne, and furious workout schedules ever piqued the coach's suspicion? Or was it easier to look the other way? "Some sports may want to do testing," says Dr. Donald Catlin, director for an NCAA drug testing agency, "but they also don't want to have too many positive results."

Perles may plead ignorance to the signs of steroid use, but the drug was prevalent on most NFL rosters during his years as a Pittsburgh Steelers assistant. As U.S. Army exercise physiologist Major James Wright, Ph.D., told the *Journal of the American Medical Association* in 1987, "Every professional football player I know takes them [steroids], with some position-related [quarter-back] exceptions." A concerned coach can almost certainly spot flagrant steroid abuse among his players. Did George Perles see what was happening around him? Or did his desire to win, coupled with past coaching experiences where the drugs were accepted, lead to an inconsistent enforcement of the values he publicly lauded—values that some MSU alumni never seemed to appreciate, anyway?

Consider, for example, what Gary Smalt, president of the West Michigan MSU Alumni Association, stated in early 1987: "That [family, education before football] is the proper atmosphere—provided we win. If he [Perles] has a 3-8 season, he could talk all he wants about God, country, and apple pie—it's not going to make a difference. The number 1 priority is beating Michigan. It doesn't matter if you use nuclear weapons, but that is a must. Number 2 is to have a winning season and bowl appearance. Number 3 is a family atmosphere of counseling a team."

With Perles' back conveniently turned to that third priority, the players bit. It's hard to blame them. "They're simply put in an environment where the rewards for success are enormous," Dr. Donald Catlin argued in the February 1990 issue of *The Physician and*

Sportsmedicine. "There are platefuls of drugs that can bring about that success, but athletes are still asked to play fair. The majority of those who succumb would be happy to stop their drug use if we could show them there was a tough, fair program weeding out the users."

♦ ♦ ♦

Pat Shurmur certainly has seen the effects of steroids. He says he never used them, but was constantly aware of others reaping what they believed to be steroid benefits. Shurmur said coaches stopped looking the other way and ignoring the problem in 1985, because steroid use became more of an issue and drug testing before Bowl games became commonplace.

"Coach Perles could see that the other guys were doing them and said, 'Listen, I don't want you guys to do them because I'm concerned about your health," recalls Shurmur. "There was drug testing internally, not just for steroids but for other drugs as well. If Coach Perles felt that you were a drug user, you were tested. And there were certain guys who were put on the 'doctor's team'—that's what they called it. And those were the guys who had a problem."

Those players who tested positive were dealt with covertly, but steroid effects are often difficult to hide. "I was never part of the steroid world, but I always suspected some things went on," Shurmur says. "I think the use of steroids becomes a mental addiction. When they're using them, they feel like they're God, and when they're off them they feel like less of an individual. People talk about 'roid rage,' and they talk about it making you aggressive. It's true that sometimes guys who are on steroids end up not controlling the drug, so they take a swing at their girlfriend or take someone on at the bar. Whereas a guy who isn't on them is pretty stable as an individual and can be a gentleman."

So the initial motive for taking the drug—to obtain a rush of strength and energy—overrides any side effects that have been documented by the medical profession. The will and desire to play and perform at peak levels is too intoxicating. But, as with all mind- or mood-altering chemicals, the high ultimately fades and the steroid "hang-over" remains. Shurmur has seen it before.

"Though they can make you a little stronger in August, the effects eventually will wear off," he says. "So later in the season they've got a real psychological thing beating on their brains. It's counterproductive. They're losing two pounds a week, and instead of thinking it's a natural process, they think they're puny or weak, so that's the way they play."

That never was a problem with Tim Moore, however. His high-intensity personality even carried over from the playing field into MSU area bars on occasion. "Tim's not a real key-to-the-city type of guy," Shurmur says. "Everybody in East Lansing knew that."

Especially those who worked in the bars. "When Moore came in, the whole bar would cringe," said a former bouncer at Dooley's. "Basically, we just tried to keep everybody away from him, instead of trying to keep him away from people. We knew any little thing was likely to set him off and there would be trouble."

Whatever others perceive Moore to be, he still wants to be a professional football player. He defends his use of steroids as a means to that end. "I find it hard to believe that people would judge me just for that one incident," he says, "just because I experimented with steroids to gain weight. Just so a pro coach would look at me. Just so he would *look* at me."

◆ ◆ ◆

Mandarich, of course, never had that problem. His downfall after the 1988 season became *how* people looked at him. His intensity after returning from the NCAA's three-game suspension earned him a sixth-place finish in the Heisman Trophy balloting, and he was eagerly awaiting the outcome of the Outland Trophy voting. The Outland Trophy is awarded annually to the country's most outstanding interior lineman, and many assumed that Mandarich was a lock. But the trophy went instead to Auburn's Tracy Rocker in front of a national television audience, and MSU and Tony Mandarich were stunned.

Many interpreted the voting as an attempt to bring Mandarich down another notch. Perhaps his image had preceded and hurt him once again.

"I think that was a big part of it," says Mandarich. "I don't think some of the voters liked me. But I think that my play spoke for itself, my ability. That's how they should decide the award: on ability. Not by what you say in the papers. [Rocker] being taken 66th in the draft and me being drafted second should tell you something."

Not long after the Spartans lost a 34-27 decision to Georgia in the Gator Bowl, a restless Mandarich decided to move as far away from collegiate life as possible. His infatuation with big-time American football—an obsession that was the sole impetus behind leaving Canada—had turned to disgust. He felt the hypocrisy of a system that considered itself pristine pure, yet exploited thousands of athletes. The NCAA had thwarted his attempt to make money off his talents before; this time, he would do it his way.

On National Signing Day in February 1989, typically a day when recruits are announced and George Perles plays Dr. Feelgood with his tales of academic responsibility, Mandarich dropped the bombshell. "Hey, did you guys hear?" the enormous presence at the door asked a roomful of reporters and an obviously embarrassed head coach. "I'm going to L.A. I'm going to meet Guns 'n Roses!"

MSU Head Coach George Perles looks on intently during a team practice in preparation for the 1983 season.

Photo by David Olds

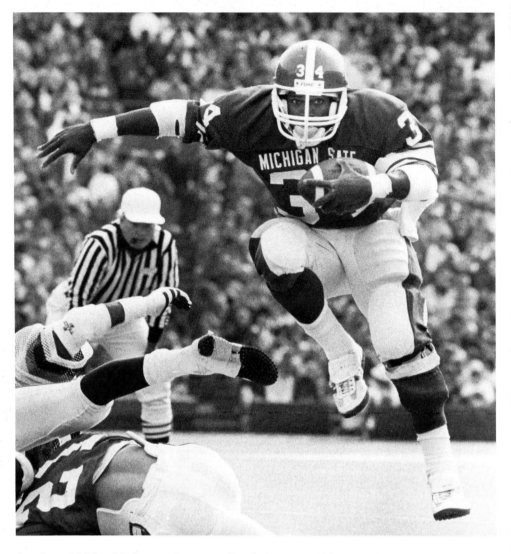

October 1986: Michigan State tailback Lorenzo White gains yardage against Purdue.

Photo by Robert Brodbeck

Facing page: MSU quarterback Bobby McAllister hands off to Hyland Hickson.

Photo by Robert Killips

November 1986: Spartan quarterback Dave Yarema (left) flips the ball to tailback Blake Ezor during the Wisconsin game.

Photo by David Olds

Stellar running back Blake Ezor shakes a tackler on a rainy day at Spartan Stadium, 1989.

Photo by Robert Killips

November 1987: Split end Andre Rison celebrates Michigan State's second touchdown against Indiana after catching a 22-yard pass in the second quarter. MSU's 27-3 victory sent the team to the Rose Bowl.

Photo by Robert Jones

Jubilant Michigan State fans tear down a goalpost after the 1987 victory over Indiana.

Photo by Robert Brodbeck

January 1988: George Perles addresses members of the media to announce he will turn down a coaching job with the Green Bay Packers and continue to coach at Michigan State University.

Photo by David Olds

At a press conference in 1990, Coach Perles fields questions about steroid use among his players.

Photo by Robert Killips

September 1988: Offensive tackle Tony Mandarich looks on during a team practice following his suspension.

Photo by David Olds

No one knew quite how to respond to this boyish ex-
uberance. Mandarich stood, grinning, wearing a black
leather jacket over his gym sweats and a baseball cap with
its brim turned backward. All Perles could do was to
tactfully suggest that his All-American take the good news
down the hall.

Mandarich wasn't bluffing, either. He had been in close
contact with the reigning Mr. America, Rory Leidelmeyer,
and was now preparing for an upcoming NFL career with
this new friend. He headed for the West Coast in March,
before winter term ended, which he knew would make
Michigan State look like little more than a football factory.
People who expressed shock at his move were simply
admitting they didn't know him at all. If they knew Mandarich, they would have realized he didn't care at all how
MSU looked.

"A lot of people bitched about me not graduating," says
Mandarich, who now concedes that "academics weren't
even on my mind" when he bolted to California. "But I
never signed a contract that said I would graduate. I just
signed for the scholarship to play football."

His eligibility over, Mandarich and his fiancée, Amber
Ligon, a former MSU student, were off for La-La Land—
which seemed a match made in heavy metal heaven. Not
surprisingly, the inevitable publicity followed hard on
their heels. Soon after Mandarich was drafted second
overall by the Packers, he referred to Green Bay as "a
village" and casually mentioned that he wanted more than
the $11.4 million the Cowboys had paid top pick Troy
Aikman. He then received an intriguing phone call.

It was Sharbaugh, his agent, calling to say he had heard
from boxing promoter Shelly Finkel. It seems Finkel and
fight trainer Lou Duva were playing around with the idea
of having Mandarich step into the ring with Mike Tyson,
who was then the heavyweight champion of the world and
the most feared human alive. "At first I thought it was a

rumor, but they flew out and gave me a workout," Mandarich says. "Lou Duva said, 'If I didn't think you could do it, I would tell you. I think you can do it.'"

But there would be a price. Duva and his son Dan told Mandarich he stood to make $5 million. Mandarich said he wouldn't do it for less than $10 million.

The widespread perception was that the fight idea was a bargaining ploy to get the Packers to sign Mandarich quickly and on his terms. A reasonable guess is that Tyson and his guardian devil, Don King, never even considered such a match-up. When Tyson alluded to the possibility, it was always in jest. So, once again, Mandarich was painted as the money-hungry monolith with a limited number of brain cells and even less class.

"Mike Tyson opens his mouth two days before his fight [with Buster Douglas] and says that he could kick my ass, Herschel Walker's ass, and Bo Jackson's ass any day we want, and then he gets into the ring and gets his ass kicked," Mandarich says. "What does that tell you? I'm telling you, that fight made people think twice about my fight. I wasn't going into that ring to box Mike Tyson. I was going in there to kick his ass. And I was going to make $10 million. As far as it not happening, I don't really think it affected anything. I just think it created more controversy."

But not as much as the *Sports Illustrated* cover story on April 24, 1989 that was published as part of the magazine's NFL draft preview. The article dealt mainly with Mandarich's voracious appetite—not only for food but for kicks. Kicks that he satisfied along the L.A. beaches with motorcycles and loud music and good times.

And, said the story, maybe steroids.

True, it was just a magazine article, but two things disturbed Mandarich: 1) it was printed in the most widely known sports publication in the world, one that many accept as gospel; and 2) it rattled something inside him as no other single piece of publicity had done before. For once, Mandarich wasn't sure if bad publicity was good publicity.

"I thought it was very two-faced. They told me how it was going to be a great article, how they were going to paint this image of a bad boy yet an all-American kid," Mandarich says. "But then it comes out, and I put myself in the place of a typical American high school kid reading this story about me. I was like, 'Well, he's cool in a way, but he's the kind of person who keeps denying he's on steroids, yet everybody says he's on them. He listens to Guns 'n Roses and rides Harley-Davidsons down the Pacific Coast Highway and lifts. That's it. That's his life.'"

Mandarich was particularly upset with two anonymous quotes—one from a Big Ten player and one from a Big Ten assistant coach—that claimed Mandarich undoubtedly used steroids. The player said: "I played against a guy who was an average offensive tackle [in 1986] and then went from 270 pounds to 300 pounds in one year and became an awesome offensive tackle. He had pimples down his arms and was next to bald."

Mandarich believes that player was former Michigan defensive tackle Mark Messner, with whom he had a tense rivalry as a collegian. "Anybody who is a coach or player in the Big Ten and is saying that without revealing who they are is a wimp," offers Mandarich. "It's probably because [Messner] got his ass kicked last year. It's because of jealousy."

Jealousy. It's a word that comes up often when Mandarich talks about his critics. After all, what other reason would cause sweet-talking John Miller—a co-captain along with Mandarich on the 1988 MSU team—to spend a large portion of his time at the Detroit Lions' training camp in 1989 ripping his former teammate? Miller felt

Mandarich's contract demands and eccentric behavior embarrassed Michigan State, and he wasn't afraid to vent those concerns, now that the hulk was safely out of sight.

"I guess that's what happpens when you don't get drafted," countered Mandarich during his holdout. "All I can do is play my violin for him."

Miller wasn't alone. Fellow offensive lineman Bub Kula's stinging comments about Mandarich that same summer angered him further. Kula has since apologized for the remarks, but the backbiting episodes clearly disturb Mandarich. Perhaps he never really believed in the lily-white image of college athletics, but his respect for the ideals of teamwork and unity were something else. That's coming from the lineman in him.

"A lot of things that Kula said could have been twisted around," Mandarich says now. "I knew Bob as a good friend . . . the kind of friend that I trained with. But when Miller came out saying things I was pissed, because I knew he was saying things that just can't be screwed up or quoted out of context by a reporter. And they were said repeatedly. I think there was some jealousy there—I was the second player taken, got the money, and had the spotlight. And he wasn't even drafted.

"He tried to apologize down the road when we played the Lions, but I didn't care—even 20 years down the road from now. I will never point a finger at one of my teammates, whether I play with him or not. It's just a rule George teaches you."

Of course, even teachers can bend the rules. Here was Perles sitting in his office during the height of the Tyson talk last spring. The subject at hand was spring practice and its rigors, but Perles—amazed at the hype and commotion generated by a lineman, the same position which had landed him a football scholarship more than 30 years earlier—couldn't help but make a crack. "We've always had some players who have played football and baseball, football and track," he paused to allow a small smile, "and some even want to box."

Perles was able to laugh at that one, but there has always been a sidelight to Mandarich that is much more serious, and which threatens the coach's entire athletic principle. It is too easy to brush aside accusations of steroid use as resulting from sheer jealousy. It's not that simple. This is a question that may forever haunt Mandarich's career: Did he use steroids or didn't he? The speculation continues from all corners.

Though he has passed five drug tests (twice through the NFL, twice at the Rose Bowl, and once at the Gator Bowl), some feel that Mandarich's dealings with Leidel-meyer and other bodybuilders have made him capable of masking his use, or timing it expertly. Indeed, the bodybuilding profession has embraced the drug for years. And with public awareness about steroids increasing, the iron-lifting fraternity has mastered ways of masking steroid use.

In the *Journal of the American Medical Association*, Purdue University's Dr. Lamb estimates that athletes and their advisors are quite adept at overcoming such barriers to drug use. Many, he says, have switched from long-lasting, more easily detected, injectable steroids to oral agents that can be eliminated from the body within a month. This research corresponds with the testimony of Jeff Case, who said Mandarich told him how to alternate oral and injected forms of the drugs and advised him when to switch to water-soluble drugs to pass an upcoming urine test. After all, if an athlete knows when a test will come—at a bowl game, for example—then he can plan ahead for that test.

The ineffectiveness of Michigan State University's probable cause drug-testing program, in which an athlete is not tested unless there are outward indications of drug abuse, is highlighted by Dr. Lamb's example of a steroid-masking regimen used by athletes for 13 weeks prior to a competition:

Weeks 1-3	*Athlete injects himself weekly with testosterone cypionate and ingests oral steroid daily.*
Weeks 4-6	*Athlete doubles the dose of testosterone and increases oral drug by 50 percent.*
Weeks 7-8	*Athlete raises doses of testosterone and oral steroid; can also "stack" a second oral preparation on top of other drugs.*
Weeks 9-10	*The dosage of injectable testosterone is reduced to make detection less likely three weeks later. Oral dose remains the same.*
Week 11	*Testosterone and first oral steroid are discontinued; human chorionic gonadotropin, a masking agent, is injected daily.*
Week 12	*The second oral steroid is gradually eliminated; final injection of masking agent is administered.*
Week 13	*No drug used.*

Leidelmeyer and Mandarich, like many weight-training fanatics, are hesitant to expound on the evils of steroids. Mandarich, in fact, defended Canadian sprinter Ben

Johnson soon after Johnson was stripped of his 1988 Olympic gold medal for using steroids. "He won the race, didn't he?" Mandarich said. "Isn't that what counts?"

Leidelmeyer, who said, "I've seen the effects of steroids, I've seen the good," offered a similar assessment of steroid use when interviewed from the Uptown Gym in Whittier, California. "It's like taking 20 gallons of gasoline and adding a pint of STP," he said. "It's enhancement. But putting 20 gallons of STP in your car and adding a pint of gasoline isn't going to do it. I put a dietary program together [for Tony Mandarich]. I put together a supplementary program based on nutritional needs, and I put together a training basis for football needs, and he responded very well."

Pat Shurmur, a lineman alongside Mandarich for three years and his coach for one, was asked recently if it would be naïve to think Mandarich had not used steroids at Michigan State University.

His answer: "Yeah, I think so."

Mandarich, of course, has repeatedly denied these allegations. Following the *News* story, Perles contended that the team routinely tested the All-American according to MSU's probable cause guidelines, finding no trace of steroid use. That attempt to silence critics, however, doesn't correspond with Mandarich's story. "I was never questioned on suspicion," he told Steve Klein of the Lansing *State Journal.* "There was no probable cause to test me." Obviously, someone is telling the truth, and someone isn't.

These blows to Mandarich's character and integrity certainly didn't prevent him from attaining two major goals. He is a professional lineman. And he is a millionaire. After missing most of the Packers' 1989 training camp, Mandarich finally signed a four-year, $4.4 million contract.

But that time away from camp—and a lack of pass-blocking training while at Michigan State—prevented Mandarich from making any kind of impact on the NFL as a rookie. After failing to crack the starting lineup and, indeed, barely seeing action in his first year for the improving Green Bay franchise, a quieter Mandarich is biding his time until he can once again play king of the hill. "I'm a die-hard Packer now," he says. "I'll do everything I can to help them out. I'm not pissing and moaning about being there now. That's where I play. All those people who said I was a flop, I'm going to show them where it's at and tell them where to shove it."

Does Mandarich still see himself as big? Of course he does. But he has found that it is possible and more prudent to please himself—and Amber Ligon, whom he will marry next May—than everybody else on the face of the earth. In fact, Mandarich even found life in L.A. to be too fast for him. He found it "distressing," and his relationship with Lindelmeyer apparently is a thing of the past. "I just think there were some things he couldn't accept, like having a 22-year-old kid on the verge of making millions of dollars," reasons Mandarich, who hasn't spoken with his mentor since July of 1989. "And I pretty much don't need his services any more."

The much-anticipated meeting with Axl Rose has also been forgotten amidst the disquieting memories of L.A. A modest plot of land in Traverse City, Michigan, Mandarich thinks, would be a better place for Amber and him to spend the off-seasons. He hopes these will be quieter off-seasons than he has lived through in the past, including this past summer, answering new steroid allegations. "Tony was a loner, basically," says Lindelmeyer with a sigh. "With his height and weight and the position he was in, he always felt he was an oddity. And, after a while, he began to enjoy it."

Until, of course, it became too big for even Terrible Tony to handle.

◆ ◆ ◆

Jeff Case, the man who branded a scarlet "S" on the Michigan State football program, nervously scans the crowd at Crossroads Cafeteria. He doesn't quite know what to expect these days. Violence? Retribution? Piercing glares? What Case does know is this: since exposing the steroid problem at Michigan State University just one week ago, he has alienated one side of his family, received 11 death threats, and moved in with his girlfriend. "It's out of fear," he admits. "I don't want to wake up one night with a shotgun at my head."

Mandarich denied the charges. He said the proof lay in his negative drug tests, and claimed Case was motivated by jealousy. "That's a poor try," Case says. "Besides, any expert steroid user knows how to time it perfectly so he'll pass the test. And that was Tony . . . he never had to worry about probable cause testing because that program was nonexistent. I never heard about them testing anybody."

And so it goes. Case went public with his story because of guilt, he says: Guilt because he had lied to his parents about using steroids. Case felt he was doing the right thing by talking about his experience. Now, Spartan-loving relatives on his mother's side of the family won't speak to him. Threats against his life—*"You're gonna f——— bleed"*— keep pouring in on his answering machine. Nights spent relaxing in area pubs are out of the question. "I can never walk into Dooley's again, that's for sure," he says.

Case, who will graduate in 1992, is preparing for an unusual remainder of his college career. When teachers call his name, students will stare. He will forever be a "marked man," because many people don't like what he had to say. They don't like the fact that he disrupted the special magic of fall Saturday afternoons. "I'm going to try to go on with life as usual, but maybe it will be a little more cautiously, a little more in the shadows," he says. "But people should know about this. Right now, we have a winning program at the expense of people. They just see the wins. They don't see the expense."

4

BRUSHES WITH THE LAW

"Don't tell George. Don't tell George."

— Spartan player Joe Bergin

Harry Wright had always believed in the legal system. He recalls those lectures as a beginning law student, the lectures detailing the way we so judiciously handle grievances in this part of the world. It wasn't perfect, of course; nothing ever is. But it was the best anywhere, Wright thought, and his experiences up until the night of October 4, 1986 only reaffirmed his faith in the fact that the legal system did, indeed, work. That's why he became a lawyer.

And on Sunday, October 5, 1986, when his brother John appeared at Wright's door hours late for a morning hunting trip, bruised and battered—the victim of an assault—legal action seemed only proper. He soon discovered, however, that this was not going to be an ordinary assault and battery case. Other factors would enter into this case, things that Harry Wright never learned about during his years at Cooley Law School. The accused

wasn't just a 21-year-old Michigan State University student; he was a football player.

It was a situation that later caused the Wrights to believe
that John's well-being, and his testimony, were taking a
back seat to another consideration: the welfare of the
Michigan State University football program. "I assumed
college athletics were something of a big business," says
Harry, speaking from his office in Owosso, Michigan, "but
I never imagined how much people would bend over back-
wards for these people. We are taught that if you break the
law, then you pay for it. You have to be responsible for your
actions. But these kids get special treatment. It's just a part
of life, I guess. But I don't think it's right."

♦ ♦ ♦

It probably wasn't the first time Mark Nichols had
cussed that day. After all, the six-foot-two, 258-pound
defensive lineman, who once likened his penchant for
punishing quarterbacks to "a gladiator going to war," had
suffered tragedy less than ten hours earlier—in the form
of a 24-21, last-second setback to Iowa. Patience and
understanding weren't his most noticeable attributes as
the night of October 4 faded into the early morning hours
of October 5. A victory that had seemed so certain had
slipped away. Now Nichols, teammate Joe Bergin, and
some friends were out to vent a little of their pent-up
frustration.

John Wright never cared much about football. He was
the night manager of Denny's Restaurant, a favorite late-
night eatery less than a mile from the Michigan State
campus, but he never became too caught up in the tri-
umphs and tragedies of the Spartan football team. So it
was with no great alarm or worry that Wright greeted the
typically raucous Saturday-night crowd. The fact that
76,000 Spartan hearts had just been broken was of no

consequence to him, at least not until 2:45 a.m. rolled around.

"That night," John says nearly four years later, "was the beginning of a long soap opera." It was also the night Wright absorbed four blows to the head, lay helplessly on the floor of the restaurant as wild kicks struck his body, suffered a slight concussion, and began to live life with a partial hearing loss in one ear. Wright says the man responsible for this offense was never charged—not because of a lack of evidence or eyewitness testimony, but rather because on Saturday afternoons the assailant happened to don a Spartan football uniform. "The police didn't want to touch this, because of who did it," says Harry Wright. "It was covered up, it's as simple as that. George Perles has got everybody in his pocket."

This is John Wright's story:

A group of seven husky men drew some attention as they entered Denny's shortly after 2:00 a.m. Before long, they were conspicuous not only because of their appearance, but also because of their abusive language. About 40 people were waiting for tables that morning, but when Mark Nichols and his friends arrived, smelling of alcohol, they walked straight back to several dirty tables at the rear of the restaurant. On their way, they passed John Wright's wife, Marcia, and her friend Elizabeth Smith, already seated at a table. According to Smith, the following exchange ensued:

Nichols: "How are you ladies doing tonight?"

Smith: "Better than you are."

According to a Meridian Township police report, Nichols then began calling the women "whores, sluts, holes in the walls." That prompted John Wright to ask the group to leave. "I don't have to take this f——— shit from you," Nichols told Wright.

As the men walked past the women's table again, Smith, who was sitting next to the aisle, claims Nichols ran into her and stepped on her toe, which was broken and bandaged. When she screamed out in pain, says Smith, Nichols lifted her up, shook her, and threw her back into the booth. When Wright protested, he says Nichols punched him, knocking him to the ground. That's when Nichols and two others began slugging him and kicking him in the head while he was down.

The abuse stopped when police were called to the scene. The officers who arrived met with two people: an aching and bleeding restaurant manager and a football player (Wright says it was Bergin) who pleaded, "Don't tell George. Don't tell George."

That is when John Wright first realized his word would not be worth much. "The police pulled me away and took me back inside," says Wright. "I wanted to press the issue and press charges, but they just wanted to let them go. I couldn't believe it. They kept on saying, 'Are you sure you want to do this? Do you know who these people are? Just let them go home.' They weren't going to write up a report."

Then, as Wright insisted they take the information, an officer added a poignant forewarning: "This may not be good for you."

What followed was an unpredictable ordeal for both John and Harry Wright. Something that seemed so simple—as simple as the concept of right versus wrong—collided with the values and needs of the MSU football program, and thus started to become very complicated. For some reason, no police report was filed on the Monday following the incident. Only after prodding from Harry Wright did the Meridian Township police finally put together a report with Wright's comments. Usually, a victim of violence is treated sympathetically by police, but not in this case. "They did not want to write it up," says Harry. Dr. Susan Roubal of the Delta Medical Center confirmed John Wright's injuries: a slight concussion, bruises on the body, and recurring headaches. Finally, there was no choice, and police wrote a report on the Tuesday after the incident, as the Wright brothers tried to negotiate with the MSU football team for compensation. "We never wanted to make it public," says Harry Wright. "We've got nothing against Michigan State University or the football team. I just wanted to make sure my brother received compensation. I mean, he could have been killed. We tried to get some sort of agreement without going to the media."

It didn't work. Greg Croxton, usually the team's man in charge of student affairs, tried to convince the Wrights to drop the charges. "If there were players involved, we'll investigate it further and work things out," Croxton told Wright on Monday. A day later, Croxton's response was similarly evasive: "We're still investigating. Give us more time." So Wright went public. The Associated Press had the story Tuesday evening.

When word reached Perles, he fumed. "I have investigated the situation, and none of my players was involved," raged the coach, who believed his team's preparation for the October 11 Michigan game was being disrupted by the allegations.

By Wednesday, police had no choice but to interrogate Nichols and Bergin for their versions of the incident. There was one problem: George Perles wouldn't allow Meridian Township Sergeant Robert Nelson access to the accused players. It was the week before the Michigan game, and media access to all players had been cut severely. But did that policy overrule a police inquiry into a possible assault? Apparently it did.

A Meridian Township police report filed on October 8 states: "Coach Perles advised us that he had several discussions with the players who were involved in the situation and he feels they are being truthful with him." In other words, the cross-examination and fact-finding process of investigative police work was done by the football coach. Perles told Sergeant Nelsen that, although Nichols and Bergin had been at Denny's the night of the assault, neither was involved in the "scuffle." In fact, Perles said, Nichols had tried to pull people away from Wright. The report ends: "Let it be noted that Coach Perles also stated that Mark Nichols and Joe Bergin do not drink."

Meanwhile, John Wright was bombarded by a strange mixture of sympathy and resentment. When the story hit the papers, the 32-year-old restaurant manager was seen as a hero of sorts, trying to buck the system. He received phone calls and letters from strangers who identified with his struggle. "I got quite a few letters," says Wright. "A girlfriend of one of the players said she was physically beaten by him, and when she went to the police they said to forget about it. About 12 to 14 people either sent letters or stopped by to encourage me, well-wishers who had tried to go up against the team through the system and who had gotten shut down. We got the farthest of anybody."

But Wright also faced the wrath of those who followed Spartan athletics blindly and failed to understand his actions. He had stuck his neck out to challenge a supposedly airtight organization, all in the name of justice— his justice. What he got were taunts. What he got were threats. His family was frightened. People wearing serpent-green jackets would saunter up to the counter at Denny's and publicly ridicule and chastise him. There would be times when an emotionally weakened Wright hid in the back office to escape the verbal abuse and the insanity.

"I couldn't believe the threats," says Wright, who still is wary of talking about the ordeal. "People I knew who would always come into Denny's suddenly turned on me. And then there were the people I never knew, but who knew who I was. They would say, 'How dare you go up against MSU? Who do you think you are?' I mean, these were business people, people I respected. It's always stuck with me, the way I was treated. I'll never be able to forget it."

The investigation continued to plod along. On the Thursday following the incident, Meridian Township police re-interviewed Wright, his wife, and Smith. All claimed that a man with curly blond hair (Nichols) was the assailant, but three employees of Denny's told police that a dark-haired man was the one throwing the punches. To Wright, this seemed like a strange thing for them to say. He claims he possessed two dozen written statements from customers pointing the blame at Nichols, but none of those witnesses was ever contacted by police.

Later that day, October 9, Ingham County Prosecutor Donald Martin charged 21-year-old Mark Hammond of Bloomfield Hills, Michigan—a dark-haired friend of Nichols who had been in East Lansing for the weekend—with the assault of John Wright.

It was then that the case began to proceed in an almost comical fashion. Here was Martin proudly announcing that the case had been solved, that Hammond was the guilty party, and that no football players had been involved in a criminal manner, while the Wrights maintained the wrong guy had been nabbed. Through it all, John Wright was never brought in to identify the suspect. It also seemed strange that Hammond's name never appeared on any Meridian Township police report leading up to a charge.

Then, with all the finality of Michigan's 27-6 drubbing of the Spartans that Saturday, the case dropped from sight. It never made the headlines again.

Several attempts to contact Martin about the affair were unsuccessful. He didn't return the calls.

Were the Wright brothers telling the truth, or were they trying to embarrass the Michigan State football program? Were they hoping that fame and fortune would follow from what they thought would be a high-profile case? Maybe.

Or could it be that the Wrights' claims were completely factual: that the MSU football program, with help from Martin, had covered up Nichols' involvement and had worked closely with police to direct the investigation accordingly?

No one dared ask if the program were that powerful.

It wasn't until a rainy evening in February 1990 that anyone bothered to inquire again about the events of October 5, 1986. Harry Wright, now running an optometry practice in Owosso, shuffled through his notes from the case and chose his words carefully as he relived the ordeal.

"There was a news blackout in East Lansing; Martin said that was it, and that was it," says Wright, who initially was reluctant to talk about the matter. "Perles has got a football team to protect, and he'll do it any way he can. He'll lie, cheat, steal, or whatever it takes. I have nothing against the man, but it makes you kind of sick—he's supposed to be a molder of young men. That's bullshit. He'll do whatever it takes, and he's got everybody in his pocket. Even Martin. Martin plays ball with MSU. He didn't want to tick anybody off; he knew what was going on.

"Why weren't we ever contacted to identify the kid they charged? It was handled so secretly. They charged him, and that was that. They made that kid a fall guy to protect Nichols. Hammond was the fall guy. We kept telling them that wasn't the one, but then we started getting letters from these lawyers in Lansing pressing for a settlement out-of-court. We figured we had taken it as far as we could. I just wanted to get something out of it for my brother, so . . . "

Wright leans over the desk to show a letter from the Lansing law office of Dykema, Gossett, Spencer, Goodnow and Trigg. It is dated November 12, 1986. In it,

attorney John B. Curcio suggests a simple and efficient
way of keeping the case out of the courts and the papers.
He suggests a settlement. The state legislature, through a
law known as MCLA 766.19, makes such restitution legal
in order to speed up the legal process. "I would like to
discuss this matter with you further, and to explore
whether MCLA 766.19 can be a vehicle for resolving this
matter on a basis which is satisfactory both to you and my
client," Curcio writes. "It seems to me that since a period
of time has elapsed, and now that passions have subsided,
we should be able to reach some sort of a reasonable
agreement."

The next question is obvious: Did the Wrights receive
a payment to drop the case? A smiling Harry Wright
refused to answer.

John Wright, however, did not refuse.

By January 1987 it was a done deal—and John Wright
was $10,000 richer. The check came from a Michigan
National Bank in Lansing, and Wright claims it was drawn
from an account the MSU football team has at the bank
for such emergencies. A copy of the five-page settlement
confirmed that the amount was for $10,000. Elizabeth
Smith, reached at her East Lansing home, also confirmed
the amount.

Who paid for the settlement? If Hammond did, why did
the check come from a Lansing bank? He was a resident
of Bloomfield Hills and never a student at Michigan State.
Wright understands what the reaction will be: Either
people will believe his story or they won't. Since there is
no legal way of tracing the check, it may never be known
who really paid for the settlement. But Wright says he
knows. "They're just going to say the kid paid for it," he
says. "They're going to lie."

♦ ♦ ♦

Times change. For whatever reason, Spartan football players are not always protected by a police shield, as in the Denny's incident. Once in a while the wall crumbles to reveal a shocking extent of lawlessness: drunken driving arrests, assaults, and violent behavior at local bars. It became known as the other side of George Perles' family, the unruly and reckless side.

An instance of this civil disorder came on October 12, 1989. An eerie and disturbing sight greeted the residents of Virginia Avenue that Saturday night. There, in an adjacent and usually empty parking lot, officers of the East Lansing Police Department gathered, donning protective vests, slipping on helmets, and making sure all riot gear was in place. This was their game-day preparation, much like the football team's methodical equipment adjustments prior to athletic clashes. It was preparation for battle. But the link between the gridiron and the padlocks didn't end there. On this night, another chapter of the storied rivalry would be added to the books. There would be another meeting of what had lately become MSU football's greatest battle: the Spartans versus the local police force.

MSU had already lost its game of the day—a heartbreaking, last-second 14-10 loss to Illinois. A planned victory party at the house of placekicker John Langeloh had been deprived of its customary enthusiasm and appeal, but revelers continued to arrive at 546 Spartan Street despite the loss, to partake in what college students quaintly refer to as a "kegger." In layman's terms, this is a party where students pay a few dollars to enter a house and drink beer supplied from an assortment of kegs. It's a common East Lansing occurrence on a Friday or Saturday night, but it is also illegal. Most nights, however, the practice goes unnoticed.

But not this Saturday night.

East Lansing police were still smarting from an embarrassing riot in the streets next to the campus following a
10-7 loss to Michigan the week before. News cameras
transmitted pictures across the state of fire, damage, and
uncontrollable MSU masses, and an ill-prepared East
Lansing police force was blamed for the situation. Now,
with a homecoming game against Illinois next on the
schedule, police promised that there would not be a repeat
performance of this mayhem. Extra officers were ordered
and given explicit instructions to be inflexible. It wasn't a
particularly good time to be flirting with illegality.

While most of the town remained calm, the 400 party-
goers at 546 Spartan overflowed into the back yard,
which prompted irritated neighbors to call the police.
"They were dressing up like they were ready for war,"
says one Virginia Street resident who observed police
slipping on their riot gear. "You could tell they weren't
going to take anything from anybody that night. They
meant business."

About 60 officers, wearing riot gear and carrying clubs,
arrived in vans and crashed the party. Langeloh and a
roommate were arrested the following Monday and
charged with selling alcohol without a license—a felony.
Langeloh, a quiet sort, appeared red-faced during his
November 20 preliminary examination and may face up
to a year in prison. Compared to past infractions of his
teammates, Langeloh's offense seems minor. "I think they
are trying to make an example of me," he told reporters.

Langeloh was hardly the first Spartan to draw attention
for his off-the-field activities. That example had already
been set by:

- Tailback Blake Ezor's two drunk-driving arrests
  and his subsequent ten day jail sentence for violat-
  ing the terms of his probation.
- Wide receiver Andre Rison's drunk-driving arrest
  in Charlotte, Michigan, on February 17, 1988. He

registered a .10 blood-alcohol level and was sentenced to a six-month probation.

- Fullback Greg Montgomery's August 1987 accident, in which he started up a construction truck that ran into a car. He was charged with a misdemeanor. Later, Montgomery was involved in a rock-throwing incident at apartments off-campus in which several windows were shattered.
- Wide receiver Mark Ingram's conviction for breaking and entering a dormitory room in 1985. He was sentenced to 30 days in jail.
- Running back Craig Johnson's connection with the unarmed robbery of a Toledo bank on April 1, 1988. A two-year investigation resulted in charges brought against the 23-year-old because his car was involved.

These illegalities culminated in the November 5, 1989 incident at Tango's, a bar in downtown Lansing. Three Michigan State football players—Carlos Marino, Travis Davis, and Bill Johnson—along with ex-football player Troy Woody and Spartan basketball player Jesse Hall, were arrested in connection with a 1:30 a.m. scuffle at the lounge. Witnesses say Johnson accosted a Tango's waitress after she declined to dance with the six-foot-five, 270-pound defensive lineman. Davis and Marino were arrested outside the Lansing police station at 3:00 a.m., when the pair tried unsuccessfully to free Johnson from prison. The final stat sheet? Johnson and Davis were charged with two counts of assault, and Marino with obstructing and resisting officers.

The waitress involved, Kim Rahar, referred to the football players as "a bunch of jerks," but said the matter had been settled. She refused to comment further.

Perles' handling of the case mirrored the Denny's incident. Though three of his players were charged with crimes, no disciplinary action followed from the top, except for tightened curfew hours. "I've done some investigating on my own, and I'm not finished looking into it," he said. In other words, no suspensions were forthcoming. Those familiar with Perles' techniques and the schedule—a key clash at Indiana was next—weren't surprised. Perles' hand was finally forced on November 8, when Marino was arrested for the second time in four days. The back-up tight end from Detroit Central was nabbed for speeding, clocked at 47 miles per hour in a 25 miles-per-hour zone, and also given a second offense for driving with a suspended license. He was suspended from the team indefinitely.

The incident was not resolved completely until May of 1990, when attorney Fred Abood, Davis, Johnson, and Woody attended a Lansing City Council meeting to publicly apologize. Each player had served 80 hours of community service in return for dropped charges. Abood, who traditionally defends Perles' players when they collide with the law, was the lone speaker. He apologized for their involvement and, in a bizarre twist, said the players planned to send Lansing Mayor Terry McKane an autographed Spartan football. The council applauded. At this point, officers involved in the case became offended, while others at the meeting were puzzled as to why the Tango's Trio were treated like celebrities. As Ingham County Prosecutor Donald Martin told one print reporter, "What the hell did they get an ovation for? They're criminals." McKane, leery of accepting the political grenade, donated the ball to a local boys and girls club.

Local bartenders aren't surprised when told of these incidents. From what they say, many MSU football players have seemed more than ready to liven up a college town with violence. "The football players drank for free; they basically had free run of the place," said a three-year employee at Mac's Bar, a popular Lansing nightspot. "They had an unlimited tab so they wouldn't cause trouble. But sometimes it would get wild in there; there were so many incidents, run-ins with bouncers. You could see [the players] didn't care. They didn't care because they knew they weren't going to get into trouble."

But sometimes they do get into trouble. Sometimes they even go to jail.

♦ ♦ ♦

Blake Ezor is either a good liar or a great drinker. He has no trouble looking his inquisitor in the eye and saying his second impaired driving arrest—the one that landed him in jail during finals week late in 1989—wasn't because of erratic behavior. Ezor, who had been nabbed in October of 1987 for his first such offense, swerved into a roadside mailbox on August 7, 1988 and registered a Breathalyzer reading of .08.

His well-publicized problems with East Lansing's finest were suddenly a hot topic again, and Ezor claims much of the friction stemmed from unfair treatment by the police.

"I'm not a murderer or anything like that," said Ezor, who alleges that a woman drove into his lane and forced him to swerve. "I could have left, I could have run, I could have said my friend was driving, but I didn't. I had had only four beers the whole night. I went up and grabbed the lady and said, 'You're gonna wait right here. We're gonna wait for the police to come.' She was a real bitch."

But when the police arrived, the officer in charge didn't seem concerned about the woman's involvement, according to Ezor. "When he showed up and saw it was me, I was going to jail if I had had a sip of beer. He didn't care what had happened. All he cared about was getting me to jail and getting a notch in his belt. It was bullshit.

"I did not swerve off the road like the papers said. I swerved off the road, not because I was drunk or fell asleep or was wasted or saw a ghost or something. It was either hit her in her car or try to miss her. I did, and I swerved through a bunch of poles, light poles, signs, and finally I ended up pinning the mailbox."

Ezor's Breathalyzer reading was difficult to dispute, however, and he spent the night in jail. He claims he was handcuffed tightly enough to be in pain, and that his pleas for relief were met with ridicule from the East Lansing police. "They said, 'You're a football player, aren't you? Can't you take it?'"

Things didn't change when they brought Ezor back to the station. "First they asked me if I liked staying in their Holiday Inn. And then, when the doors would open, they'd say, 'Blake Ezor, come on down!' like on *The Price is Right.* They didn't have to do that. 'How's George gonna like this?' they'd say. I mean, it seemed like it was fun for them to ruin my life."

Ezor, who had been cited for moped violations before the impaired-driving convictions, was dealt with "internally" by Perles, and was allowed to fully participate in the 1988 season.

"Blake had some problems," said Pat Shurmur. "I don't know if he was selfish or what, but some of the things he did were very dumb. My editorial on that is that he was very lucky he played at a place where George was coach. George gave him chance after chance after chance to come back. And if you look at Blake now, he's matured a great deal."

The local media still questioned Perles' leniency, and Ezor received hundreds of letters criticizing his behavior.

"I got stuff from Michigan people saying, 'Bo wouldn't take that. You'd be off the team,'" Ezor said before the 1989 season. "Well, Bo kicked off that fullback [Leroy Hoard] and then brought him right back. So don't tell me about Bo. I'm on Coach Perles' probation, not on Bo's. People still send me letters, and Coach gets them, too. He tells me, 'Don't even worry about it.' And I don't."

Even so, Blake's father Bernie (a former casino pit boss who met Perles during a Super Bowl celebration at Las Vegas' Aladdin Hotel) moved in with Blake before the '89 season to keep a closer eye on his son.

Ezor claimed his father was not the only one watching. He compares his situation in East Lansing with that of former basketball standout Scott Skiles, whose two drunk-driving arrests almost cost him his senior season. Like Skiles, Ezor claims, he was discriminated against by policemen who wanted to embarrass him.

"One time I came out of my house and there was a cop parked out in front with his lights off, and this was at night," he says. "He followed me when I left." Another time, Ezor says, he was stopped at a light on Lake Lansing Road when a policeman recognized him, ran across the street, and said, "Let me see your license." The policeman then yelled across the street for his partner to run a check on Ezor, which proved negative.

"You get a label, and it just spreads," says former Spartan fullback Steve Montgomery, one of Ezor's close friends. "That's what Blake has had to deal with, being in the limelight. No one has to read anything. They just see the name and make their own assumptions."

It appears they may have assumed the worst about Blake Ezor. They have assumed he is a threat to society. Whether or not that is true, Ezor served nine days for the second impaired-driving offense and would like to prove he and other MSU football players can work hard to respect society's laws. But the jury is still out.

"OK, I made a mistake," he said. "Thank God I didn't kill a person. But, I've learned from it. They should tell you, 'Hey, you're going to be a role model—watch what you do.' I never even realized that before."

◆ ◆ ◆

Perhaps the most disturbing part of these brushes with the law is the message sent from the top, the message sent from Perles. Or rather, the *lack* of a message.

Throughout this book we have seen George Perles continue to sacrifice integrity to field a winning team. Here again, a precedent has been set allowing MSU players to commit any offense and still expect to be in the lineup the following Saturday. It has happened with Blake Ezor, Travis Davis, and John Langeloh. It will happen again unless Perles changes his disciplinary system.

Whenever his athletes are involved in legal matters, Perles shields them with the following response: "We're handling it internally." Hence, the player ends up on the field come game day because, supposedly, Perles has already punished him. The obvious question remains: What sort of disciplinary action deters such displays of lawlessness? At Michigan State University, it seems as though no action is taken.

It is not that way at other schools. The University of Michigan, for example, suspended hockey defenseman Todd Copeland for several games during the 1990 season for causing a disturbance outside a sorority house. Perles' toleration is clearly the exception, not the rule—and is quite frankly frowned upon by his peers. "We in athletics can't say 'Boys will be boys' and that athletics are combative and competitive—I don't believe in that," Minnesota Athletic Director Rick Bay told the Lansing *State Journal* shortly after the scuffle at Tango's. "We're supposed to be in the field of academics and help young people keep their lives in proper perspective. And that means they have to function in public."

Too often, there are players who don't. The nightlife of East Lansing becomes merely an extension of the football field, where brawn and muscle are placed above any law or value. And, if no real discipline is forthcoming from the program, then it's very difficult for the players to learn otherwise. It is not enough to say that kicking restaurant managers or roughing up waitresses is wrong. That slap on the wrist rings hollow when an athlete is then allowed to scamper on a football field bearing the proud name of Michigan State University days after spending a night in jail.

Perles' curfew punishment is insulting to the general public, which is directly affected by his players' crimes. He continuously raves about the quality of the "kids" inside the Spartan system, and yet refuses to make that a position of honor. His reluctance to suspend arrested players pushes each member of the program further away from being a completely respected member of society. They all become less than exemplary, less than a source of pride to the university proper.

Following Ezor's second drunken-driving arrest in August 1988, Perles said he was clamping down on the tailback. "Blake's walking on eggs now," he gloated. Come September 10, there was Ezor walking not on eggs, but onto the field—to play a football game against Rutgers. Perhaps if Perles had sat the tailback down for a game, Ezor wouldn't have been tempted to risk his future two years later when he pulled his price tag switch. The time to discipline, to positively hold his personality, came and Perles watched it go by. While every athlete surely should be allowed a second or even a third chance in life, there comes a time when the line must be drawn. The game can't be that important.

Or can it?

"It's a sick mess over there," says Harry Wright. "Everyone is bending over backward to protect those guys. I just don't get it."

5

1986: THE PASS

"To this day I'll still go out and when I see people they'll say, 'Hey Dave, how's it going?' And then they'll say, 'Boy, that Iowa game.'"

– Former Spartan quarterback
Dave Yarema

The reality of it all didn't sink in until days after The Pass. After the teasing, the barbs, the reporters' questions, the scornful looks. He had experienced all those before. Every quarterback has.

The letters were what really created the pain. Hateful letters. They poured in after The Pass, those unmerciful reminders of a moment that some people—and certainly the man responsible—will never forget. And the more letters he peeled open, the more it became clear these weren't mere "games" he was playing any longer. Dave Yarema, a 21-year old college student who happened to play quarterback on his school's football team, discovered exactly how high the stakes were in the game he was playing. They were stakes he had never bargained for.

111

"People sent me letters. One guy called me the devil," he says with a nervous chuckle. "Honest. The guy was a lawyer. He signed his name and everything. He said George Perles was the devil, and I was the devil's son."

Yarema paused, creased a piece of pizza in his hand, and looked at his visitor. "It freaked me out."

He wasn't the only one. The Pass has become deeply embedded in Michigan State football lore. It sits there, uncomfortably, beside the other noteworthy eponyms in Spartan history, such as Duffy, The Tie, and Biggie. It would prefer to drift silently away from memory, but the emotion involved was too strong. And too real. There's no mythology or embellishment in the events of October 4, 1986. Though a fulfilling Rose Bowl victory and two other post-season appearances followed, The Pass remains the single most memorable play of George Perles' years in East Lansing.

The vision of Yarema, three yards from the school's biggest win in a decade, rolling right in a Spartan Stadium dimmed by impending sunset, looking for an open man through the drizzle before finally snapping his arm back and floating the ball gently into the arms of Iowa's Ken Sims, will always be there. It will never fade.

"There were thousands of fans screaming," Perles said two years later. "And then—silence."

To fully comprehend the demoralizing nature of the Spartans' 24-21 loss that afternoon requires an understanding of the events leading up to The Pass and, equally important, the atmosphere of the moment. Spartan Stadium was buzzing with electricity, and with good reason. It was the return of big-time college football to East Lansing: national television, a serious Heisman candidate, a Top 20 ranking. For the first time since Darryl Rogers left town in 1979, the Spartans talked Rose Bowl and weren't laughed at. But the renaissance of a dormant power was facing a critical test against undefeated Iowa.

The script couldn't have been drafted any better. Here were the Spartans, trailing by three, darting down the field against the defending Big Ten champs in the game's closing minutes. Leading the drive with precision passing was Yarema. The fifth-year quarterback already had passed for 271 yards and three touchdowns. He was poised to become just the fourth player in Spartan history to throw four scoring passes in one game. As the ball sat on the Hawkeyes' three-yard line with 1:32 left, punching it in appeared a mere formality. The win would announce that the Perles era had arrived.

But it never came.

"That play killed everything," Yarema says. "It was rough. To this day, it's still tough. That thing changed my life. I mean, national TV, everybody who I had ever known in my life watching. People freaked out, man."

Seriously, now. Who didn't?

♦ ♦ ♦

East Lansing in early September is usually calm. Classes don't begin until the end of the month, so the student population hasn't yet made its presence felt. The streets are relatively bare, and the trees along the Red Cedar River are quietly beginning their colorful metamorphosis. The strained sounds of the marching band practicing on Landon Field can be heard, and there is, of course, the thumping of pads nearby at the Duffy Daugherty Football Building. No one usually paid much attention, though. In recent years this football business had been considered something of a futile preoccupation. From 1966 to 1983, no Spartan team went to a Bowl game. Sure, there were big wins—Ohio State in 1974 and the 1978 Michigan game—but for the most part, national prominence wasn't within reach. Besides, the state belonged to Bo Schembechler and Michigan.

That all changed in 1986. Or, at least, it was supposed to change. Earlier in the decade, Illinois and Iowa had successfully broken through the Michigan–Ohio State lock on Pasadena invitations, and now it appeared that Michigan State was next. The Spartans, coming off a 7-5 year, were loaded offensively. Of the starting 11, five were destined to go on to the National Football League. Mark Ingram and Andre Rison were extraordinary wide receivers and posed the biggest headache for secondary coaches in the league. Senior fullback Bobby Morse was an expert blocker, while Tony Mandarich began molding his legend on the offensive line. Then, of course, there was "Lo."

Tailback Lorenzo White had captured the hearts of fans and the fascination of Spartan coaches with a remarkable year in 1985. The soft-spoken sophomore from Fort Lauderdale, Florida led the nation in rushing with 2,066 yards in 12 games, finished fourth in the Heisman Trophy balloting, and earned unanimous All-American honors in a high-profile position. White single-handedly put Michigan State University back on the map. He survived, without injury, an incredibly demanding workload in 1985—419 carries (nearly 35 per game)— and was expected to produce the same astronomical numbers again as a junior. This time, the stakes would be higher; White was to carry the reborn Spartans to the promised land.

Before beginning that storybook trek, however, there was first the task of accommodating a deluge of preseason speculation and predictions. No longer were the Spartans a harmless little Saturday afternoon diversion for mid-Michigan. Suddenly, they were national news: grist for the *Sports Illustrated* mill and every other publication infatuated with Top 20 material. Crossroads Cafeteria, the on-campus site of Perles' season-opening press conference September 8, was packed with members of the news media scribbling down everything the coach and his Heisman candidate had to say—which wasn't much. This was new territory for both. Perles proceeded cautiously, careful not to anger his rivals, and added another cliché to his growing collection. "We're low-keying it," he said.

Meanwhile, White was visibly unnerved by the tape recorders, microphones, notepads, and questions. Repetitious Heisman inquiries bordered on the absurd, and White patiently tried to answer each one, which only seemed to make matters worse. His hushed tones forced reporters to crowd in even closer, greatly adding to the tension. No Michigan State player had ever won the coveted Heisman, and White represented the school's best odds in history. One look at the media guide, which devoted four full pages to White, was proof of that. His success on the field translated into a responsibility off the field, whether he liked it or not.

Perles had stumbled upon something not even hated Michigan had—a marquee running back—and he wasn't about to let the advantages go to waste. White represented a way to sell tickets, and he fueled an unbridled optimism about the Spartans that had not existed for what seemed an eternity. A painful lesson would soon be realized, however: Dreams don't come true overnight. Michigan State began the 1986 season on the verge of a breakthrough. It ended the season dangerously near a breakdown.

"That was the toughest season I've ever been through on a team," says Craig Johnson, whose goal-line fumble at Northwestern capped a season of frustration. The loss in Evanston was the Spartans' fourth three-point loss of the year. They were numbers that would be repeated often. Four losses. Twelve points. That's what stood between a major bowl bid and heartbreak.

The preseason glitter began peeling away as early as the first game, played at eventual PAC-10 champion

Arizona State. White was held to 61 yards rushing, and his fourth-quarter fumble led to the Sun Devils' game-winning field goal in a 20-17 heartbreaker. It also served as a harbinger for Yarema's curious fate, as he completed 26 of 33 passes for 256 yards but failed in the game's final minute. The Spartans sat on the Arizona State eight-yard line with under a minute remaining. Any hopes of a touchdown were drowned as Yarema was sacked from behind on a roll-out, and much-maligned placekicker Chris Caudell's subsequent 34-yard field goal to tie the game was blocked by Darren Willis. End of story.

The Spartans flew back to East Lansing to await a date with Notre Dame and its second straight national television broadcast. The Fighting Irish, under first-year coach Lou Holtz, were also dragging after a 24-23 loss to Michigan. When these two titans met it was under gray skies, and they played an even grayer game. The afternoon's only drama came courtesy of Spartan cornerback Todd Krumm, whose 44-yard interception return for a touchdown in the first quarter put MSU ahead to stay. Krumm also delivered the fatal blow by picking off a Steve Beuerlein pass with 1:31 left in the game, preserving a 20-15 win—Notre Dame's first loss at Spartan Stadium since 1968. "We're breaking down those records now," Perles said. "We keep achieving things that haven't been done since the sixties."

Following the Spartans' 45-10 whipping of Western Michigan University, anticipation was soaring. White, with 400 yards rushing through three games, was back on a Heisman pace. With CBS' cameras returning to East Lansing to telecast the Big Ten opener against Iowa, the season of destiny appeared to be in full bloom, primarily because the MSU attack now had an option other than the quick pitch to Lorenzo. It had the arm of Dave Yarema.

The quarterback from Birmingham Brother Rice had waited a long time for this moment, and he deserved some reward for his patience and the struggles he had endured. Yarema had come to Michigan State as one of Muddy Waters' final recruits in 1982, and was immediately thrown into action as a 17-year-old trying to save a 2-9 team from disaster. When Perles took command a year later, he looked to Yarema to lead the turnaround. Yarema struggled to stay healthy, however. A broken thumb in the 1985 season opener caused him to miss five games. The Spartans went 6-0 with Yarema calling the signals, but were 1-4 with freshman Bobby McAllister at the helm. Perles knew that a fit Yarema was the key to any breakthrough year, and Yarema appreciated the restoration job Perles had done at MSU. That was the extent of conciliation, though, in their point–counterpoint football relationship. The kid wanted to pass; the coach wanted to run. So the Spartans ran.

"You can't come right out and say you're really unhappy," reasons Yarema, whose admiration for Perles overshadows any difference in theory. "When you're a quarterback and you're starting, you want to throw the ball. To be successful, you have to have a mix. I never said, 'I disagree.' The only thing I did was when I thought that I saw something that looked good, I changed plays. Whenever I said I wanted to do something different, he would always listen. I respected him for that. But up until my senior year, we just had a running game."

Yarema, who wound up leading the Big Ten in passing in 1986, was determined not to let his final season waste away with a prehistoric game plan. He tired of seeing nine defenders on the line of scrimmage to stuff the running game, and he emerged in the preseason ready to do what he believed should be done. "We're going to throw the ball this year, I can feel it," he said after the spring game. "We can run the ball and go 7-4 again. If you run, you're going to beat the mediocre teams, but not the ones you need to beat as a contender."

So far, his change in mindset had worked. Yarema threw for 277 yards and two touchdowns against Western Michigan and appeared poised to do the same against the Hawkeyes, who were forced to start at quarterback a reserve named Tom Poholsky, whose collegiate experience totaled all of eight passes. But the Spartans were full of mistakes this day. Fullback James Moore fumbled a kickoff return, penalties erased crucial first downs in the second half, and with MSU trailing 21-14 with ten minutes remaining in the game, a roughing-the-kicker penalty on Paul Bobbitt led to the Hawkeyes' final field goal—ultimately the difference in the game. "We have no business running into the kicker when you have a bad angle like that," said a livid Perles. "That was a mistake, and there were a number of mistakes."

Perhaps the biggest flub of all was a fourth-quarter screen pass to White, who caught it and was hit square on the knee by a Hawkeye. He left with just 41 yards and would never be the same again. "If I could bring back one play, it would be the screen pass," Perles would say after the season. "It'll be a cold day before Lorenzo catches another."

Still, Yarema's arm almost made folks forget about the mistakes. With four minutes left and MSU down by ten, Yarema rolled to his left, threw across his body while falling down under heavy pressure, and hit Mark Ingram for an eight-yard touchdown pass to bring the Spartans within three, at 24-21. Iowa was stopped on three plays, and MSU had the ball again and began marching toward a storybook ending—until the story's final page was torn out.

Yarema never looked better as the Spartans moved easily into scoring position. His final completion of the day, to Ingram, pushed the Spartans within three yards of victory. But there were several circumstances for Perles and his staff to consider: 1) MSU's Heisman candidate,

White, was on the sideline with a sprained knee; 2) MSU's top receiver, Ingram, was on the sideline repairing his torn jersey; and 3) MSU had one time-out and 1:32 left to play. Perles decided to call for a roll-out. The coach who didn't like to throw would fool them all with a pass. As Perles sent Yarema out with the play, he added, "If it's not there, throw it away."

"I wanted to guarantee that we had a chance to get in that end zone four times," Perles said. But one chance was all they got.

The intended receiver was tight end Rich Gicewicz, but he was pulled down by his face mask, leaving only one player, Mike Sargent, in the pattern. "I didn't really know what happened at the time, except that I got pulled down," Gicewicz recalls. "I didn't realize until I saw the films that it was that flagrant." Yarema continued rolling right, looking for Gicewicz. He could have thrown the ball away, or possibly have run for the score. Instead, he saw Sargent open for a moment, and threw the ball.

"I thought when I threw it, we were going to win the game—that's why I threw it," a fatigued Yarema said afterward. The play was so cataclysmic, so improbable, that even the Hawkeyes left the field wondering if they had just been on the receiving end of divine intervention. "I want you to know that you are probably blessed," Iowa's coach Hayden Fry told his team afterwards in his Southern-fried accent, "because the good Lord just reached down and touched me, and maybe some of it has rubbed off on you."

Meanwhile, the Michigan State postgame interview room resembled a morgue, with everyone waiting for Yarema. He spent 30 minutes surrounded by reporters in a cramped and cold corridor inside Spartan Stadium, staring into the lights of cameras, reworking the play in his mind, and trying to figure out what he had just done with the flick of the wrist.

When he was through explaining the inexplicable,
Yarema walked into the lonely dusk a different individual.
The Dave Yarema who had entered the stadium that
morning was everything the 1986 Spartans had become;
he was brash and confident, looking forward to events to
come. It was a Dave Yarema who would never return.

Neither would that team. For this loss affected more
than Yarema's psyche; it destroyed a team not well
schooled in the delicate art of accepting defeat. With the
Michigan game looming just seven days away, a quick
recovery was necessary, but not likely. "It hurt the whole
season," Perles said two years after The Pass. "I've never
seen a team try to recover from such a loss. It was a tough
one mentally. It hurt the following week. It hurt the entire
year."

It hurts even today. "If only I could have stayed up—I
kind of take the blame for the whole loss," Gicewicz says.
"It was a devastating loss."

With devastating consequences.

◆ ◆ ◆

Perhaps it wouldn't be fair to pin the blame on a single
source. Was it the fault of the fans? The coaches? How
about the media? In retrospect, this really isn't important.
Regardless of the culprit, no matter where the injustice
was born, the damage had been done. One troubling fact
remained: Sometime during the span of 11 games, Dave
Yarema lost the drive, the courage, and the will to be a
quarterback. The boyhood fun of it had vanished. Now,
more than three seasons removed from the hell that was
1986, Yarema still does not know why.

"Hey, I just tried to have fun through the whole thing,"
says Yarema, who hasn't strapped on a helmet in nearly
three years. "I lost the edge. I lost that burning desire. You
have to be crazy. You have to want it bad. I lost that, I
really did. I lost it quick, too. I don't know. I mean, a lot

of those guys are animals, just superhuman beings, in the pros."

Yarema smiles. He recalls his tryout with the Green Bay Packers and a stint in arena football. It all seems so long ago. "I'll tell you something; I like sitting in the stands," he says. "There's a lot of pressure out there. Pressure just playing. It's nice to sit back and watch."

Yarema looks comfortable in his new role, but not much is different. He sips a beer in Dooley's, an East Lansing bar, his short brown hair still parted in the middle. He was left behind in the school's Rose Bowl party, which came a year after his eligibility was finished. There was no time for fans to forgive, to understand. Instead, he was on the outside looking in. For most fans, as quickly and emotionally as the 1987 Spartans brought them the title, Dave Yarema had given it away.

"I lived through it, and it was rough," he says. "Of any person at the stadium that day, you would have wanted to be anyone but me. Afterward, going to class, I'd be sitting there, and they'd be staring at me. That was tough, man. That was a tough time in my life. That game, I felt I played a great game. It was one of my best. Nobody remembers that."

No, just The Pass. Because Yarema resided in a college town—where students, professors, and residents interact with athletes on a regular basis—the reminders were constant. It was a bizarre education for an athlete who had always reaped the benefits of college athletics. Now, he was seeing the darker side, the inordinate importance placed on these games played by so-called amateurs. In the end, Yarema may have learned more from this experience than from his academic experience.

"I just had to realize that it's something that happens," says Yarema, who graduated in March 1987 with a communications degree. "It changed me. It may sound funny, but looking back it was a good experience to go through.

It was tough. I always thought of myself as kind of humble, but when you're a quarterback here for five years, you get kind of big-headed. It humbled me a lot, man. It was very humbling."

Even so, Yarema doesn't have much patience for the critics. "It's like people have never been through anything," he says. "They don't know what it's all about. One thing I learned here is that you can never criticize anybody. I go to the games and hear people yelling, 'George, what are you doing? You stink.' It's like they don't know what they are talking about."

The abuse did affect Yarema, not only off the field but on it. Though he left as Michigan State's all-time leading passer, the National Football League wasn't particularly interested. He wasn't even drafted, crippling a confidence level that already was none too high. Yarema signed a free-agent contract with the Packers, but was cut before the season began. "When I was up there I wanted to make it, but I felt funny the whole time," he says. "I didn't feel like I was there all together."

He tried to hook on with the Detroit Drive of the newly born Arena Football League in the summer of 1987, but a torn rotator cuff in his first preseason game ended that dream. Two shoulder surgeries sapped any remaining desire to play football. Yarema's competitive drive was dead.

Indeed, teammates noticed a new Yarema almost immediately after the Iowa debacle. He not only felt like he had let down his team, but also that he had stalled the maturation of an entire program. "There are fans out there—Michigan State fans—and they don't realize that they are doing a lot of damage," Johnson says. "Dave was a great leader. He would always come out yelling, getting us fired up. But after that pass, he just didn't have that fire in his eyes any longer. He probably could have been a great one."

Instead, he was just an above-average collegiate quarterback and nothing else. That's more than most recruits can say, and Yarema is satisfied with that lot in life. He's content working for his father's business. The game is past now, and he doesn't mind one bit.

"The pressure never really bothered me," he says, a touch of the old competitive flair returning, "but you kind of get burned out on the whole thing when you do it your whole life. I don't miss it as much as I thought I would."

♦ ♦ ♦

It had been longer than 24 hours. In fact, it was closer to 72. Yet, when Perles walked into his weekly press conference on Tuesday of Michigan Week, he still sported a look of confusion. The talk, understandably, didn't revolve around knocking the socks off Michigan, but rather about how an injured team with only three fifth-year seniors could recover emotionally before Saturday. Answer: It couldn't.

Still, Perles and his players heroically tried to convince everyone that the 24-hour rule—that any Spartan game, win or lose, is forgotten by the following Monday's prac-tice—had done the trick. "Before you get healthy physical-ly, you have to get healthy emotionally," Perles said. "It was a tough defeat, but it only lasts a short period of time because the next game keeps getting bigger and bigger." Added White, "You have to put the losses in the back of your head and start to play."

The only problem was, White wouldn't play. His sprained knee was worse than first thought. He missed the next two games and carried the ball only 54 times the rest of the year. The Heisman hopes were a bust. Next to White in the trainer's room was MSU's top offensive lineman, Doug Rogers, also a sprained knee casualty. So the damage was physical as well as emotional, and the Spartans were faced with the laborious task of winning in

Ann Arbor short-handed, or dipping below the .500 mark at 2-3.

The man counted on to pick up the slack was White's roommate, the little-used Craig Johnson. The back-up tailback from Massilon, Ohio certainly had talent to contribute, but he had never broken into the one-back offense. His most vital contribution to the program in two and a half years had been to help White memorize his plays. Now, he was expected to run them against one of the nation's top rushing defenses, even though he had had just 19 minutes of playing time in the season's first four games.

Johnson was respectable—20 rushes for 81 yards—but his teammates were not. The Wolverines crushed MSU, 27-6, and also battered Yarema, who was helpless behind a shuffled offensive line. "Physically, I got abused out there," recalls Yarema. "I got beat up. They kept blitzing." On the rare occasion Yarema did have time to throw, speedsters Rison and Ingram were bottled up. The receiving duo combined for just one catch.

The optimism that had dominated the preseason now had been completely deflated. The raw reality that transforming cellar dwellers to champions doesn't occur overnight began to sink in, and it hurt. "I told you guys that we weren't ready yet, but nobody listened," a scornful Perles told his weekly press gathering. "I never said we were. I'll let you know when we are."

The season wasn't over, of course. There were still six games remaining, and past history suggested a Bowl bid wasn't out of the question. In 1985, MSU saved a 2-4 start by winning its last five Big Ten games and going to the All-American Bowl. So hope still flowed from an uninspiring 2-3 beginning. All it would take was six straight wins.

The trek began in Champaign, Illinois. Fullback Bobby Morse ran for two touchdowns and Johnson added 96 yards rushing as the Spartans cruised to a 29-21 win over a sub-par Illinois team. "We plan on winning our next five games," senior linebacker Shane Bullough said afterward.

Two more wins not only revived interest in the team, but also seemed to foreshadow a decent Bowl appearance for the Spartans. MSU clobbered Purdue, 37-3, as White returned to action with 79 yards rushing. Then came the revitalization of the passing attack in the Metrodome in Minneapolis. Yarema threw for 321 yards and three touchdowns on 25 of 30 passes as the Spartans beat Minnesota, 52-23. "Everybody had a lot of fun out there today," Yarema said. "In my mind, I'm thinking 'Bowl game.' You know, a lot of people say you can't think Bowl game yet. But I'm a senior, and the Bowl game is in the back of my mind."

It was on everybody's mind. After all, the Spartans were now at 5-3. White left early with a bad ankle, but the game marked the emergence of a tough-nosed running back named Blake Ezor, who rushed for 107 yards. A New Year's Day Bowl game wasn't out of the question—until Indiana arrived the following week.

As seven Bowl representatives crowded the Spartan Stadium press box, MSU fell behind 14-0 and lost to Indiana, 17-14. James Moore had apparently saved the lackluster showing by blocking Dan Stryzinski's punt with 1:19 remaining. The ball rolled to the eight-yard line and the crowd waited for Yarema to punch the ball across. But the ghosts of Arizona State and Iowa resurfaced. Morse was stopped for no gain on first down, and then Yarema was sacked for a ten-yard loss setting up a third-and-goal from the 18. Yarema dropped back to pass, saw Ingram open at the goal line, and threw the ball. It was intercepted. "I zipped it in there. I zipped the ball," Yarema said apologetically. "I guess the luck's not going our way. I don't know what happened."

Neither did Perles. "It's hard to explain why you have letdowns," he said. "It's difficult for coaches to get the kind of feeling that there's going to be a letdown."

Obviously. Because the same thing happened seven days later, this time at lowly Northwestern. The abyss came in the form of a 24-21 loss to the Wildcats, blowing any outside chance for postseason play. "Try losing to Northwestern and coming back to this campus," Yarema says, three years after the fact. "I don't know how we got beat that game. There's no way we should have lost to them. No way. There's no way with the caliber of our team compared to theirs, you know?"

A shell-shocked Spartan team wandered aimlessly about their locker room following the game. There were no tears, just blank stares. "That's a poor game to lose," said Perles, who couldn't comprehend the concept of blowing a Bowl bid in, of all places, Evanston, Illinois. Nobody could, really. White, who played sparingly on a tender ankle, just collapsed on the Spartan bench, head sunk down beneath his knees, as the final seconds ticked away. The bricks of Perles' foundation were crumbling around him, and Johnson's fumble at the one-yard line served as a scapegoat for the program's troubles. He was benched for the season finale and never carried the ball again. It may not have been an answer for all the team's woes, but it satisfied Perles. Which is all that mattered when it came to Craig Johnson.

◆ ◆ ◆

Craig Johnson, Jr. is carrying the ball. He starts underneath the stairs and picks up steam around the coffee table, until he plops on the couch, football and all. Paydirt. The two-year-old looks at his father and smiles. Dad nods his head in approval.

"I love this little guy," says 23-year-old Craig Johnson, Sr. "I can't wait until he's ready to go to college, so I can tell him what to watch out for. Then, with what I went through, it will all have been worth it."

It is impossible to expect every recruit to become a major contributor in a football program. Some won't see any game action at all, but the very least any athlete can expect is honesty. During the recruiting season, it is the coach who promises and the athlete who listens. Craig Johnson says he listened to promises that never came true.

When an unhappy Johnson requested a transfer from MSU in the winter of 1986, Perles scrambled to keep the Spartans' fastest player and save his three years of eligibility. He promised Johnson playing time. No matter that he had offered the same promise before the 1985 season, and that Johnson had listened, which effectively appeased him until the reality of just 32 carries in seven games returned the crisis to square one. Now Johnson, a 19-year-old seeing his football dreams wasting away, applied for a transfer. Arizona State and Maryland were interested. Johnson once again had hope.

But his dreams didn't correspond to those of George Perles, who was more concerned about depth charts than personal tranquility. Besides, the prospect of Johnson becoming a star elsewhere would open the MSU staff to unnecessary criticism. So again Perles promised playing time. And again Johnson listened. At the 1986 season opener at Arizona State, the kid who had turned down two schools never stepped on the field.

Johnson was crushed. "After this whole meeting, they had me stay there, and I did not play at all," he says. "They were alternating me at first-team tailback during fall practice, so I was ready. They never even told me I wasn't playing. I did not step on the field, not even for special teams. At halftime, I had tears in my eyes. I had been deceived. I was so hurt. I could have gone somewhere else. So the team runs out for the second half, and I just stood there. That was the worst feeling I've ever had. It was unbelievable how they would lie to me and not play me at all. I was wounded, man. Wounded."

Johnson, of course, would get his chance later in the season as White struggled with injuries. He gained 345 yards on 78 rushes—a respectable 4.4 per-carry average—but was switched to defensive back for his junior year in 1987. He played sparingly. Then, with his senior year and, finally, a starting position approaching, defensive coordinator Nick Saban, the man who entered Johnson's Canton home talking about MSU's inside route to the NFL, accepted a position with the Houston Oilers. After Saban left, secondary coach Dino Folino redesigned the depth charts, moving Johnson to back-up cornerback. Another promise had been stripped away. It was the final one. "I just said, 'I don't need this,'" he explains. "There were all kinds of rumors that I flunked out, whatever. I just didn't want to play any more. That's it. The day I quit Michigan State was one of the best days of my life."

But who exactly is Craig Johnson? Three months after this interview, Johnson was charged with the unarmed robbery of $3,561 from Ohio Citizens Bank in Toledo on April 1, 1988. The two-year investigation centered around a license plate number for a Ford Mustang called in following the robbery. The car was registered to Craig Johnson. "He was a talented football player, but Craig had his problems," former teammate Pat Shurmur said. "He had more than one chance, more than two chances, more than three chances. There are just some people who don't take well to help people are trying to give them. It's just that he had different priorities, and they were priorities that George felt didn't fit well with those for himself or the rest of the team." Meanwhile, teammate Derrick Reed sympathizes with the pain Johnson suffered. "He was just in a bad situation," says Reed, one of Johnson's closest friends at MSU. "It's bad that they switched him all around

like that. He easily should have been starting. But football
wasn't what made us friends. We were friends whether he
was playing or not. Craig Johnson is a good person."

The point being that when Craig Johnson had listened
to recruiter after recruiter who visited his home, making
promise after promise, a dangerous thought had been
implanted in a young mind. It never dawned on Johnson
that the same pitch, the same promises, were used on 25
other recruits. When he arrived at Michigan State and
discovered he was just a single cog in a giant factory, he
felt betrayed. In truth, it was merely the reality of big-time
college football, rather than betrayal, splashing him in the
face. A cold reality that makes its way into few recruiting
visits and into even fewer young minds.

Today, Johnson still has visions of a professional
career. He played cornerback for the Canadian Football
League's Toronto Argonauts before a torn Achilles tendon
ended his season. On a snowy January day in Canton,
Johnson, fresh from his midnight security job shift at a
local can company, remains chipper. He was married in
the summer of 1990 and talks of finishing his degree
someday. "I can't afford it now," he says. "The jobs I've
had are just paying the bills." Johnson looks at his son,
once again hurtling toward the couch, and he thinks about
how much simpler the game was at that age.

♦ ♦ ♦

The season-ending win over Wisconsin was anticlimac-
tic, but Perles and his team took pride in it anyway. It was
the only thing left. With the 23-13 victory, MSU ended the
year at 6-5, not a particularly spectacular mark. But it
represented the first time the Spartans had enjoyed three
straight winning seasons since 1961–1963. The year
began with dreams of Pasadena and ended with the
nightmare of Northwestern. "The kids mostly played for

themselves," Perles said. "It's nice to have three straight winning seasons, and we'll build on that."

Still, the breakthrough year broke apart. Though everything came together one season later, Yarema wouldn't be there to enjoy it. He would be left with unwanted memories and a desire to bring back time.

"We had some good games and some bad games," Yarema says. "The Iowa game, that's what people remember. That one play killed everything. It really did."

6

1987: ROSES ARE GREEN

"I just wanted to be a part of a team that everybody would remember."

– Spartan safety John Miller

When Bobby McAllister desperately flung his body into the cool California air during the fourth quarter of a January 1988 Rose Bowl thriller tied at 17-17, two damaging perceptions of the Michigan State football program existed.

By the time he landed, they were gone.

The Spartans, it was widely believed, could neither pass the ball nor win the big games that make a school a national power. They were pretenders to a diminished Big Ten throne; they used an unimaginative offense to capture an uninspiring conference title. But here were the symbolically statuesque mountains rising above the Pasadena dusk, and here was McAllister at his own 30-yard line, running out of room at the right sideline on third-and-eight, being chased by a bloodthirsty Southern Cal defense. It almost seemed as if the beleaguered quarterback didn't spot a receiver until he was already in the air, twisting and searching and praying. When he finally did hurl the ball downfield to magical split end Andre Rison, it was at the last possible moment he could have done so. Some said the pass came out of nowhere, but it most definitely came from McAllister's heart.

The result was a 36-yard gain instead of a punting situation, and the miracle led to a John Langeloh field goal and a 20-17 victory. Michigan State University, after holding off a late USC charge, had claimed its first Rose Bowl triumph since 1956, and George Perles' promise of respectability within five years had proven perfectly prophetic. "These guys have bailed me out of a promise I made a long time ago," said Perles.

Michigan State football had rather fittingly chosen a warm-weather setting in which to "get hot" again. For the first time since Duffy Daugherty retired in 1972, the Spartans were in vogue.

"It wasn't all that spectacular to me," says McAllister of the play. "I guess it was different because people don't see that sort of thing that often, and they see long passes a lot. But it feels good, I guess, to make history and all that."

McAllister's nonchalance typified the manner in which Perles and his Spartans approached their fantastic voyage to Pasadena. It was just such a business-as-usual attitude that allowed the West to be won. All season long, Perles had proclaimed, "They all count one," whether edging Michigan or beating up on Wisconsin. It sounded stupid, but in the end this static preparedness for each and every contest was an extremely valuable asset.

The Big Ten's Rose Bowl jinx in this granddaddy-of-them-all road game was well-documented: Michigan's Bo Schembechler took ten teams to Pasadena during his career and emerged victorious just twice. The Wolverine philosophy always seemed to entail downplaying not the game, but the traditional festivities surrounding the event.

Perles, always willing to contradict a Schembechler philosophy to draw more attention to his own, opted for a looser approach. He decided to play up the social aspect of Rose Bowl Week to deflect attention and pressure away from what would be Michigan State's second meeting with USC that season. The Spartans were rarely seen around the environs of the Newporter Resort, a luxury hotel which served as team headquarters. They did the Disneyland thing, and much was made of Perles' excitement at finally meeting Mickey Mouse and Goofy. They gorged themselves on red meat and splashed each other during poolside television interviews.

In short, they didn't take themselves or the Rose Bowl too seriously. That is, until it was time to play football.

"You have to remember the kind of kids we have," said Perles a week after the victory, when the excitement had settled down and recruiting concerns had taken over. "Our players had the right attitude. They were able to handle it. You can do all sorts of preparation this and motivational that, but you've got to have the kids. As it turned out, our kids were three points better than theirs.

"We said that if we did lose the football game, it wouldn't be from playing away from home. If we got beat, we would have gotten beat by a better team."

While the Trojans were not better than the Spartans, they had improved drastically since opening the season at Spartan Stadium on Labor Day night, September 7, 1987. The Michigan State athletic department termed this first night game in Spartan history a "Great American Celebration," complete with fireworks and an elaborate halftime show. The evening more closely approximated an ostentatious proclamation that Michigan State University had decided to "go big-time."

With the chill of excitement in the air and the third-largest crowd in Spartan history in the stands, Perles' strongest team since he arrived on campus stood little chance of losing. Heisman Trophy candidate Lorenzo White, coming off a frustrating 1986 campaign, rushed for 111 yards and two touchdowns, leading the Spartans to a 27-13 win. Asked about a possible rematch in the Rose Bowl, outspoken USC linebacker Marcus Cotton said, "Yeah, if they make it. We'll be there."

By the time the Spartans had completed their non-conference schedule, however, a Rose Bowl berth seemed unlikely. Their second game of the season was another nighttime affair, a nationally televised game at Notre Dame. It was the night Blake Ezor took the opening kickoff at the one-yard line and then stepped back into the end zone to down the ball for a safety. It also was the night Irish flanker Tim Brown went a long way toward winning his eventual Heisman Trophy. He ran through and around the Spartans for punt-return touchdowns of 71 and 66 yards during the first quarter, making the score 19-0, and virtually eliminating the possibility of a Spartan comeback. Notre Dame had beaten Michigan and MSU on successive Saturdays. "We don't have our heads down," Perles said after the game. "We know we made some mistakes. We got beat as a team and the better team won tonight."

But it was the following Saturday's home game against Florida State that brought Michigan State quickly and painfully back to earth after their fantasy win on Labor Day. Early Friday morning, Duffy Daugherty had died, the victim of kidney failure at age 72, and the walls were closing in on Perles. Not only did he have to consider life without his long-time mentor and friend, but he had to find a way to slow down one of the most talented teams in the nation. "That was my fault," then-athletic director Doug Weaver said of the match-up with the Seminoles. "These things are set up ten years in advance. Who was to know they'd be that good?"

Before the 31-3 onslaught was over, Michigan State's reputation as a boring and ground-based offensive team was born. McAllister completed just four of 17 passes for 43 yards and was sacked six times, for a total loss of 50 yards. Meanwhile, Florida State racked up 24 second-half points to pull away from the sluggish Spartans. When Perles' television show was promoted by the public address announcer near the end of the game, a spirited chorus of "boos" rained down on a man who had promised great things to a town that had been more than willing to listen. Now, though, the Spartans were 1-2 and were obviously on a rung below perennial national powers like Florida State. Surely the offense was, with McAllister playing like a confused man and White held to under 100 yards.

The next week became a crucial test of the team's psychological makeup. It would have been easy for the Spartans to join the masses and allow that great enemy of successful football programs, doubt, to creep into their consciousness as they prepared to travel to Iowa. But George Perles knew better than anybody that he possessed two trump cards in his hand that hadn't been played. One was the fact that Big Ten conference play hadn't yet begun. Indeed, he could be 0-3 or 3-0 at this point and still have the same opportunity to make a run for the roses. Perles instructed his team that playing such a murderous non-league schedule was a blessing, that they wouldn't face opposition as strong as Notre Dame and Florida State for the rest of the season. In effect, they had seen the worst of it.

Perles' other trump card was his Stunt 4-3 defense, which he had molded in the same manner that made Pittsburgh's Steel Curtain infamous. Guys like Mark Nichols, Travis Davis, Tim Moore, Percy Snow, Joe Bergin, and John Miller would make or break MSU's Big Ten season—and the coaches knew these warriors had not lost their confidence or their edge. It was a brilliant run-prevention defense, one that eventually led the nation in that category and finished second in total defense. Though Notre Dame and Florida State had rushed for 168 and 180 yards respectively, surely those were not outrageous numbers from teams so loaded with ability (the Seminoles' highly touted duo of Sammie Smith and Dexter Carter was held to 47 yards). "Even though we got beat badly, they really didn't run all over us," said Nichols, a senior defensive lineman who made up for a lack of physical ability with sheer hate. "It was a learning experience. It got us ready. We knew it was going to be like that."

The unit had been taught early by Perles and defensive coordinator Nick Saban that you never give up on the system. If the tiniest bit of apprehension grew inside one player, it could spread until it made the entire defense vulnerable. Perles had designed the Stunt 4-3 after seeing O.J. Simpson run wild in a 1974 AFC semifinal game against the Steelers. Although Pittsburgh won that game and went on to win its first of four Super Bowls, Perles spent the following week devising a way to let All-Pro middle linebacker Jack Lambert concentrate solely on tackling the ball carrier. So often, it seemed, Lambert was too busy warding off offensive linemen to get to the play. "We stopped slanting our off-side tackle after that," said Perles, who at the time was Pittsburgh's defensive line coach. Instead, the linemen concentrated on keeping blockers away from Lambert, whose production increased instantly.

The Stunt 4-3 is a simple defense that can work wonders for a team that has a big-time middle linebacker. The Spartans had sophomore Percy Snow, who as a senior would win both the Butkus and Lombardi awards. "The beauty of it," said Perles, "is that you've got a guy who's free, and the ball carrier knows that. Now, when

Percy gets there—and the good Lord blessed him with this—he just unloads." As much as this scheme thrived on power, it still required poise. With all the administrative duties that eat away at a head coach's time, Perles realized that he would have to pass on the intricacies of the Stunt 4-3 to someone who had more time to teach it to the players. After going without a defensive coordinator during the 1983 season, he chose feisty defensive backs coach Saban to take charge of defensive starting in 1984. It was Saban who received much of the credit for making the Spartans such a defensive power in 1987.

"George spent a lot of time teaching us the scheme, all the details of it, and then I think we had to go with that and adjust some things to college football," Saban said. "We stuck with it to the point where the players understood it, and we didn't change our defense." The players always had confidence in Saban, whose verbosity and wide-ranging vocabulary made Spartan practices X-rated at times.

"He sure doesn't have any problem getting his message across," Nichols said after a particularly grueling workout. Every time Saban grabbed a player by the jersey, threw helmets across the field, or questioned someone's sexual preference in front of the team, it showed how bitterly he strove for perfection. That commitment rubbed off on the defense, which grew into a seldom-satiated unit known as Gang Green.

"It was an attitude, man," explained linebacker Tim Moore. "We all had an attitude. We just wanted to kick ass, you know. It's the greatest feeling in the world when a team can't run against you. I never really cared about the offense—none of us guys on defense did. We let the coaches worry about the offense."

The offense, to be sure, was still a concern when the Spartans invaded Iowa City for a game that would turn around MSU's season and send it on a westward path.

White rushed for 104 yards and a touchdown in the first half, but his fumble late in the second quarter put the Spartans in a 14-7 halftime hole. Sensing the season slipping away, Perles blistered his players in the locker room, challenging them to recall their goals and rise to attain them. A year later, defensive end John Budde was still shaking his head about that speech. "It fired us up as a team," Budde said. "I think you really need your coach to go crazy every once in a while. It showed how much he wanted to win. I was surprised at the way he said it, but I liked what he had to say."

The entire Spartan team must have liked what he said. The defense shut out the Hawkeyes in the second half, holding them to minus-47 yards rushing, and the offense began to click. After two Langeloh field goals, McAllister's eight-yard touchdown pass to tight end Mike Sargent gave Michigan State a 19-14 victory. It may have been the Spartan's biggest triumph of the season, considering a loss may have sent them reeling into oblivion. The school's most murderous schedule in history didn't get any easier, though: Michigan was coming to town. "I always thought that was the worst possible type of schedule," says Pat Shurmur, who was a senior at the time. "Because how the Iowa game went and how the Michigan game went was how the whole season went. If you look at '86, we had Iowa beat—it was a big win—and then it slipped out from under us. So instead of knowing you're a good team, you go and play a good Michigan team with doubts. I mean, it's almost impossible. Now, the Rose Bowl year, we beat Iowa and we go into the Michigan game thinking we're a pretty damn good team."

The Wolverines came in on a cloudy day, ready to throw the football, something that proved dangerous with junior quarterback Demetrius Brown at the helm. White scored two first-half touchdowns to stake MSU a 14-3 lead, and Brown's attempts to pass Michigan back into the ball game kept falling into the wrong hands. The Spartan secondary was playing a zone that allowed safeties John Miller and Todd Krumm to get to balls that were slow in reaching their targets. With a visibly pressured and frustrated Brown leading the Wolverines on national television, it became a field day. "It just seemed like the ball was floating through the air all day long," said Miller, who had spurned Schembechler and signed with Michigan State in 1985 as a top-rated recruit. "I could tell you every coverage we were in, and where Brown was looking." Miller pulled in a school-record four interceptions from his strong safety position, but it was Harlon Banett's pickoff in Spartan territory with little time left that sent East Lansing into a frenzy.

MSU had beaten the Wolverines back in 1984, but many felt the Spartans had used a slingshot to slay their mighty rival that season. It was the way this victory looked that made it such an ideological triumph for Perles and, indeed, for the university. The Spartans had dominated Michigan; there were no gimmicks, no lucky bounces. When Schembechler's team needed to score, it simply was not able to. Many Michigan State followers took this as a sign that there was, finally, equity between the state's two major-college football programs. Beating Iowa was for the body; this one was for the soul. After all, Michigan State University had not beaten the Wolverines at Spartan Stadium since 1969, Schembechler's first season in Ann Arbor. With this victory, a team that had seemed down-and-out two weeks earlier was sparkling at 3-2 and staring Pasadena right in the face. But at least one star on the MSU team had seen happier times.

◆ ◆ ◆

Finally, Lorenzo White is free. He is with three buddies at a swimming pool inside one of Michigan State's intramural buildings, splashing about with joyous innocence. It is June, so the pool is nearly empty. But the 22-year-old, who has just been selected in the first round of the National Football League draft, doesn't mind. In fact, he welcomes it. This is his time.

Resting along the south end of the pool, his arm draped over the wet tile, White sees a familiar reporter approaching. After some small talk, the acquaintance asks about White's chances with his new team, the Houston Oilers.

"Well, I have the utmost respect for Mike Rozier. I'm going to try my best," says White, who, now aware he is talking to a member of the news media, swims away to rejoin his friends.

College is supposed to be a time of inquiry, a time to ask questions. Lorenzo White never had time to ask many questions at Michigan State—he was too busy answering them.

Perhaps no other athlete in Spartan history was subjected to more scrutiny or verbal badgering than Lorenzo White, who generally seemed to feel quite uncomfortable talking about himself. So, one must wonder: What exactly was the purpose of White's college experience? Was it for him to earn a degree? Probably not. Through June 1990, White had not completed his requirements in communications, and that is not really surprising. Much of his off-field time was spent with reporters, not in classrooms. Was it to develop himself into a professional talent? Maybe, but White was often asked to carry a heavy load. There were eight games in which White ran the ball more than 39 times, greatly increasing his chance of injury. One pop in the knee is all it takes to end an athletic career. White seemed willing to pull the Perles sleigh as far as his body allowed, even when the star tailback asked to be rested. Was it to promote Michigan State football? That seems to be the most likely explanation.

"We were a team trying to rebuild, and with Perles coming from the NFL, they thought the way you rebuild was to get a star," reasons Craig Johnson. "You have to have a player that everyone wants to see in order to build hype. The way you build hype is by promoting someone. They used him as the person to build a program around. How do you get recruits? You say 'Michigan State,' 'Lorenzo White,' and 'Heisman candidate.'

"Coming out of high school, and I don't care where you're from, if you hear of a school up for the Heisman, then you want to go there. Lorenzo was used to show recruits that they publicize their players. You knew you could get publicity if you went to Michigan State."

Thus, White became less a vital offensive weapon—competent tailbacks were in abundance on the Spartan bench—than a priceless item with which to inform the nation that Michigan State football had returned. If the youngster happened to run into the ground in the process, so be it. "He would always say, 'Hey, I like running the ball, but 50 times?'" remembers Johnson, who spent many nights talking with a physically drained White. "He'd tell the coach that 50 times was a bit much. So next time out, it would be even more."

No one really expected 4,887 yards of productivity from the five-foot-eleven, 211-pound tailback when he first arrived from Ft. Lauderdale's Dillard High School in 1984. His resumé, which included 19 touchdowns en route to being named Florida's prep player of the year in 1983, was impressive, yet it didn't suggest the fame he would attain almost instantly. But when senior Carl Butler limped off the field in the 1984 season opener, it was White whom Perles summoned. He started the final three games his rookie year, and White's 665-yard season placed him clearly in the Number 1 tailback slot for 1985.

White didn't disappoint. Only once in 12 starts was he held under 100 yards (against Michigan), and "The White Knights" brigade was born. At times, the numbers almost defied logic and belief. At Indiana, White rushed for 286 yards, despite exiting shortly after halftime. He ran for 2,066 yards in all—the most ever by a sophomore—and finished fourth in the Heisman Trophy balloting.

Perles had discovered a star, a durable tailback to anchor his new regime. White's work wasn't done when he left the field, however; it was only beginning. While Michigan State wouldn't promote White as some publicity-hungry schools might—with matchbooks, posters, hats—it did expect its new star to be accessible to the media.

There was, of course, one hitch in this grand plan: White was an extremely shy individual and didn't really care for the publicity. His job, he thought, was to play football. Suddenly he was being told his job was to relate, and to relate clearly and provocatively. White was told this would increase his chances of winning the Heisman. "By doing all these interviews, I have a chance to win," White said softly, before the 1986 campaign. He averaged nine interviews a week that summer. For a Tony Mandarich, that sort of attention might have been fun, but for a soft-spoken White, it was nothing less than terrifying. Meanwhile, the coaching staff told White the sweating was worth it. "We think he is a humble guy who will take the publicity," Perles said. "He's handling it well. We'll cut him off at the start of fall camp, and then all the promoting will be done by us."

That cutoff point never came. Instead, weekly hour-long news conferences were established for White to meet with reporters. Every Tuesday, media members would cram into the rickety sports information office in Linton Hall to wait their turn. Most were told to come back the following week.

Soon, the wear on White's psyche became noticeable. Questions about his two-year-old daughter living in Florida upset an already delicate equilibrium. One Tuesday, with a half-dozen reporters waiting for his entrance, White played hooky, causing a small panic at Linton Hall. Assistant Sports Information Director Mike Pearson, who is now Sports Information Director at Illinois, frantically drove around campus trying to locate the missing Heisman candidate. One hour later he returned, empty-handed. "I don't know where he is," Pearson said tersely. "I guess we'll have to cancel it for this week."

The reprieve lasted only one week, and the interviews continued through White's disappointing, injury-ridden junior year and his glorious, 1,572-yard exit in 1987. At the year-end banquet celebrating the Big Ten championship, White stood at the podium and addressed the crowd of 1,000 admiring Spartan fans. He was still nervous, but on this occasion he spoke clearly and confidently. The kid hadn't ditched his shell entirely, but it was open wider, exposing him to more people than ever before. Otis Gray, Dillard High School's football coach, says White returned to Ft. Lauderdale a new person.

"When Lorenzo left here, he was talkative to us but not to people outside," says Gray, who has also delivered another tailback, Hyland Hickson, to Michigan State. "He knew he was going to have to open up and communicate better. I think one of the best things Coach Perles did was set him up in one of those speech classes. It did a great job. They knew he was going to have to deal with the public, and I give Michigan State a lot of credit for doing that. It was a big, big difference from the way he was when he left here."

There came a time, however, when the whole Heisman hassle began to scramble the priorities. White started blocking out the coaches' wishes and focusing on what he thought was best for him. The two didn't mesh. Finally, he asked himself whether it was worth it to sacrifice his peace of mind for the publicity produced by the interviews. Anyone with his statistics would be an NFL first-rounder, whether he did one interview or a thousand.

White wondered why his treatment changed during his senior year, and why certain of his privileges suddenly vanished. In the past, according to Johnson, White's airfare to see his daughter in Ft. Lauderdale had been paid by the MSU football program, a violation of NCAA rules. Now, with White a senior, MSU wasn't willing to take that risk anymore, and that was hard for White to accept.

"He felt he was being used the whole time," says Johnson. "His senior year, he finally realized that they didn't care about him. And he was hurt by that. He was hurt. They wouldn't be needing him next year, so they started treating him a little differently. He had requested they let him go home for some reason, and they wouldn't let him go. Any time before when he asked to go home, they had been paying for his flights. Things started changing.

"That was the first time I saw him hurt like that, but I knew it was coming. Before, when he got hurt physically, it was, 'OK, sit on the side.' That senior year, they had an attitude. They said, 'Yeah, right. Get back out there.'"

White did not return calls to be interviewed for this book, but that's really no surprise. He had fulfilled his quota long ago. Now White has requested that his current team, the Houston Oilers, trade him to a place where he can be happy.

Maybe some day he will find that place.

♦ ♦ ♦

The defense continued to dominate when the Spartans visited Northwestern, a team that had made Perles' program look silly the year before with a 24-21 upset. Cinderella never even got to the ball on this Saturday, though; she was intercepted and beaten well before midnight. Northwestern was held to 51 yards rushing and 139 total yards in tiny Dyche Stadium, which had never seemed so gloomy. Groups of huddled students watched as the Spartans rolled up 21 second-half points to secure a 38-0 rout, Michigan State's first shutout since 1985. "We knew what we had to do and we did it," said Davis. "We just wanted to beat 'em, and beat 'em bad."

That goal proved unattainable when Illinois coach Mike White brought his bandits into Spartan Stadium the following Saturday to try to disrupt Michigan State's rise into the conference hierarchy. White, who was fired after the season for maintaining a program so corrupt it forced the university to reassess its entire athletic philosophy, had taken the Illini to the 1984 Rose Bowl, shattering the Michigan and Ohio State monopoly on power. He figured that Perles matching that achievement would make it less grandiose.

So, during a steady downpour that seemed to suit the Illini just fine, the 17-point underdogs threw the ball 44 times and gained two scores through the air. They galloped around like kids under a sprinkler, taunting and ridiculing the Spartans, who once again were having trouble moving the football. Lorenzo White was being held to just 67 yards, so McAllister began to create things on his own. Chased all day from a fragile pocket by Illini defenders, McAllister set up his own fourth-quarter touchdown with a 34-yard scramble, and the Spartans tied the score at 14-14 with 4:52 to play.

When MSU free safety Todd Krumm stepped in front of a Scott Mohr pass with 38 seconds left and took it to the Illinois 15-yard line, it appeared that a fated team had narrowly beaten a hated one. "As the boss," Coach White said, "it's my dominant opinion that we didn't deserve to lose." The Illini didn't lose. They tied. Langeloh's kick was painfully low, which turned out to be the only thing that crawled between Michigan State and a perfect Big Ten record in 1987. The freshman walked into a busy interview room after the game, and at first everybody ignored him. Nobody knew who he was. He looked like a little boy lost in a supermarket. "I don't know what happened," Langeloh finally said. "I must have hit it low. I just don't know."

But a monumental win at Ohio Stadium seven days later on a crisp Halloween afternoon made people forget the Illinois debacle forever. The realities rose above the Midwestern dusk and the 90,000 people who witnessed the MSU victory: McAllister was mature, suddenly, capable of leading this team anywhere; and the Spartans were going to the Rose Bowl. Nobody said the latter, but everyone was feeling it. Though Indiana was close behind MSU at 4-1, the Hoosiers would have to visit Spartan Stadium in two weeks. And they wouldn't score many points. Not against this defense.

The Buckeye offense had scored on a 79-yard pass to Everett Ross on the game's first play, and remained silent for the rest of the afternoon. Coach Earle Bruce watched in horror as his team rushed for just two yards and threw for 145. The Buckeyes, who lost to Michigan State for the first time since 1974, managed just six first downs. Davis, who had been told by Coach Bruce as a high school senior that he wasn't good enough to play at Ohio State, sacked quarterback Tom Tupa five times for a total loss of 37 yards. McAllister continued to take off when granted the opportunity, rushing for a team-high 83 yards while throwing for only 61.

This would never be a great passing team, conceded offensive coordinator Morris Watts, so he set out to make it an extraordinary running team. That meant adding McAllister as a weapon and teaching him when and where to let his talents take over. "Early in the season, he'd always want to roll deep or go wide with the football, but

I think he's only done that once or twice in the last three weeks," Watts said a few days after the team returned from Columbus. "Now when he pulls it in and takes off, he's getting positive yardage every time. In situations where he was causing us trouble before, now he's making the big play for us."

The big plays continued during a 45-3 blowout of Purdue, which was held to minus-18 yards rushing and fell behind 21-0 during the first quarter. The Spartan running attack was effective enough to get two players above 100 yards: Lorenzo White with 141 and sophomore Blake Ezor with 151. Suddenly, the fulfillment of East Lansing's wildest football dreams was just one victory away. Instead of a traditional Michigan–Ohio State run for the roses, Perles would host Bill Mallory and his surprising Indiana Hoosiers at Spartan Stadium on November 14. "The championship game is back in Michigan," Perles told a captive media audience after dismantling Purdue, "but it's a week early and there are two new teams."

Derrick Reed had arrived at Michigan State before this season from Southern Methodist University, which had received the death penalty from the NCAA. The starting cornerback remembers being both awed and impressed by the anticipation that pervaded East Lansing in the days leading up to the game. "I hadn't been there for all the troubles and losing records that Michigan State fans suffered through," he says. "But the fans were so excited it made me feel like, 'Wow, I'm part of something that hasn't happened up here for a long time.'" Not since Darryl Rogers' 1978 team went 7-1, in fact, had the Spartans captured a Big Ten title. But that team had stayed home, haunted by the spectre of NCAA probation brought about by former coach Denny Stoltz's staff. A win over Indiana would send Michigan State to the Rose Bowl for the first time since Duffy Daugherty's powerful 1965 team suffered a 14-12 loss to UCLA—and a lot of energy had been stored up during the 22-year wait.

When the magical Saturday finally arrived (and it seemed to some that it would never materialize, that someone would pinch a football-crazy town and force it to awaken from its California dreaming), the outcome was never really in question. The questions revolved around not "what if," but "when." When would the Hoosiers' sorry fate be sealed, and when would be a suitable time to tear down the goalposts that had stood—stoic, mocking—for too long? Not before Lorenzo White was finished rushing the ball 56 times for 292 yards in what was his Spartan Stadium swan song. Even late in the game, with the Spartans holding what would be the winning margin of 27-3, Perles spoke to White on the sideline and told him the game was still his, that he should keep running.

Perles and White still clung to faint Heisman hopes, but it was more than that. They were going to try to wipe away all the pain of trampled expectations with one glorious performance by the best running back in the history of the school. White, of course, would sit at the Downtown Coaches Club several weeks later and watch the Heisman go to Tim Brown, but he had almost single-handedly assured the Spartans of this victory for the ages.

Heralded Hoosier tailback Anthony Thompson was held to just 23 of Indiana's 33 rushing yards, and Mallory's team wasn't good enough to hurt Michigan State through the air. The Spartans' 17-3 lead was more than enough to secure the championship, and when the second half mercifully ended, it seemed like all of East Lansing was present, instantly, on the magic carpet where history had been made. A bird's-eye view would have been puzzling: Certainly this was a jubilant, powerful mob, but what was it celebrating? What was its cause? With the goalposts devastated and not a single inch of the playing field visible, all signs of football had vanished.

Inside the Spartan locker room, Mallory had silenced a private celebration by storming in and respectfully addressing his rivals. He exhorted George Perles and his troops to do what Big Ten teams had so often failed to do, a failure that stigmatized the conference as weak or inferior. He asked them to win the Rose Bowl.

Indeed, that goal was the focal point of campus life in the three weeks that followed. Never had so many people stood up and claimed a Michigan State University football team as their own. "I've been in football long enough to know that's the way things are," a smiling Perles said early one morning during this euphoric period. "When you win, everybody loves you." In 1983, Perles had promised that Michigan State football would return to prominence in five years, and now the Spartans had. He was a hero, and was richer for it. Donations to the Ralph Young Fund, which funnels its assets into the athletic department, had risen more than $1 million since 1983; season ticket sales had increased by 16,000.

Of course, everyone also felt the need to display their newfound gridiron devotion. During these weeks leading up to the Rose Bowl, every day in East Lansing was St. Patrick's Day. "I see a lot of crazy people," said Connie McAuliffe, who runs the campus bookstore and estimates that his sales increased 300 percent in the midst of this hysteria. "People think nothing of coming from Canada or Detroit just to buy a shirt. One weekday, we sold twice as much as our best football Saturday ever, when we have 76,000 people in the stands." Thirteen planes were chartered by the Michigan State University Alumni Association to transport 4,600 alumni west, the largest such migration in Big Ten history. In addition, about 4,000 students joined this emotional crusade, bringing with them their rather unique approach to life. As tradition-drenched and stately as the Rose Bowl often seems, this one was going to be a party.

The festivities continued even after the RVs were enclosed in the parking lot and the huge stadium filled with expectant spectators. Perhaps there is no athletic playing surface more noble or perfect than that of the Rose Bowl, but Perles' laid-back approach to the affair helped the Spartans view it as plain old grass. They didn't seem intimidated. After an early USC field goal, White faked and powered his way into the end zone twice to stake Michigan State a 14-3 halftime lead. It wasn't until the second half that the PAC-10's traditional New Year's Day dominance seemed ready to become a factor. Quarterback Rodney Peete was getting some time to survey the field, and his strong and accurate arm began picking apart the Spartan secondary. "I think Rodney played his heart out," said first-year Trojan coach Larry Smith. "I think he played as hard as he could."

When Peete found Ken Henry for a 33-yard touchdown pass with ten minutes left in the third quarter, MSU's lead was just 14-10. "At the end of the third quarter and the beginning of the fourth, we were in deep trouble," Perles said later. "We were in bad shape." The Spartans got a boost from Langeloh's 40-yard fourth-quarter field goal, but four minutes later Peete found Henry again for a 22-yard scoring strike that tied the score at 17. Suddenly, the biggest Spartan football affair in more than two decades was completely up for grabs, and Perles' team began searching, pleading, for miracles. When McAllister left the ground in favor of the western air on third-and-eight with 7:41 remaining, they got one. Nobody would gaze at Michigan State football in quite the same manner ever again. "I just wanted to be part of a team that everybody would remember," John Miller said. "That's what I've done. Twenty or 30 years from now, people are going to look back and say, 'That's the team that started it all.'"

7

1988: 0-4-1

"It's not the Rose Bowl, it's not the Super Bowl, it's not the All-American Bowl, and it's not the Orange Bowl. It's the Gator Bowl, a classy bowl. And if anybody says anything bad about the Gator Bowl, I'm going to punch them in the nose."

– George Perles, November 19, 1988

Before Rutgers, before linemen were suspended for mailing letters to the NFL, before injuries coupled with coaching changes brought the defense back to earth, and long before opposing teams publicly linked Michigan State to steroid use, Spartan football gloriously basked in the glow of its Rose Bowl victory. It was, in essence, the talk of the Midwest.

The sweet afterglow of Pasadena spawned a close examination of George Perles' fabled foundation, which had delivered a Big Ten title in five years, exactly on cue. Just how did he do it? Perles' Stunt 4-3 defense drew a good portion of the credit, as did his ability to recruit and develop talent to fill specific problem areas, such as the offensive line and the running game. The metamorphosis from slouch to champion was also embodied in the Michigan State football home, a slick, expensive, and high-tech factory built to produce a winning program.

A walk around the Duffy Daugherty Football Building leaves one impression: Someone must love Michigan State football. Someone important. It's plain and simple. When George Perles arrived at Michigan State in 1983 to revive a comatose program, he compiled a list of necessities to compete with the perennial Big Ten powers at Michigan, Ohio State, and Iowa. MSU Athletic Director Doug Weaver responded.

"I've never been turned down by the administration," says Perles. "[We've gotten] everything we need to do the job: equipment, budget, facilities, assistant coaches, anything. Doug Weaver has never said no to me. I'd like to clarify that by saying I haven't asked for anything ridiculous. But if anyone has a beautiful situation, they can only tie us. There is nothing I need." He may be the only person on campus able to make that statement.

The Duffy Daugherty Football Building is not simply a place to practice. It represents today's state-of-the-art program—and the excesses that presently scar collegiate athletics. While the university struggles to fund departments like natural sciences, which was scrapped last fall without an ounce of public outcry, and faculty members swallow the reality that their paychecks are among the Big Ten's lowest and tuition continues its insane ascension toward the heavens and students spend hours in cramped halls outside the Student Aid Office, there is one spot on campus where economics isn't a worry.

The Daugherty Building sits prominently on the south end of campus, basking in the shadow of a 76,000-seat shrine called Spartan Stadium. It stands as a strange little exception in a hemisphere of financial strife, a place where every request—from an extra helmet to a $3.8 million indoor facility—is met. The Perles era has seen the construction of that expensive practice field, the expansion of the quarter-million dollar weight room, and a medically advanced training room. And, of course, a Big Ten Championship. The motto is clear: If you want the best, get the best, at any expense.

"It's really a very, very outstanding complex," says Lefty Smith, director of Notre Dame's Loftus Sports Facility. "If I were a football coach, it would impress me. The football staff has its meeting rooms, film rooms, everything under one roof." A mere building can't put a football program over the top, yet multimillion-dollar facilities are popping up around campuses everywhere. Clearly, coaches feel they are a ticket to success.

"Facilities don't win games," says Perles, who saw the hapless Pittsburgh Steelers move into regal Three Rivers Stadium in 1970 and proceed to win four Super Bowls that decade. "But they put players in a frame of mind where they know we are supporting them. It sends a message that we are first class." First class translated into first place in 1987. For that year, at least, the building served its purpose.

Before any game can be won, however, there is a first step: getting the players on the field. That is where Bob Knickerbocker becomes as valuable as a good nanny. Each day, Michigan State's coordinator of athletic equipment makes sure more than 130 players are dressed and ready for practice. It is here, in an office deep within the piles of shoulder pads, shoes, and jerseys, where Knickerbocker holds court. If someone needs a new knee pad, they come to Knickerbocker. A helmet adjustment? It's Knickerbocker. He supervises the outfitting of every Spartan sport, but football is the nucleus of the operation. That's easy to conclude from the pair of elongated golf carts used to lug around blocking sleds, and two condors (rising photo decks) used to film practice. "Those are nice," Knickerbocker says. "That's the way it is here. Doug Weaver has been great to us. It goes down as far as I am. I'm never told no. I don't get things just to get them, but when we need something, it's here."

Those are extras, though. Knickerbocker estimates the bill to dress each player is $285. The wardrobe includes a helmet, two practice jerseys, shoulder pads, thigh pads, knee pads, and four pairs of shoes. Pads to protect various other body parts such as elbows, hands, forearms, and ribs raise the price further. "And that's just to get them on the practice field," Knickerbocker says. Add another $110 for game-day jerseys and pants.

Each year, Knickerbocker orders $100,000 worth of new equipment. That exorbitant figure is explained by the premise that they must be ready for any situation. Look, for example, at the 700 pairs of shoes. There's a shoe for artificial turf, damp weather, the indoor facility, and grass. It all adds up. "You have to order that much," says Knickerbocker. "The helmets don't last forever, the shoulder pads, the thigh pads can wear out. You don't always buy new jerseys, but [in 1988] we did. If we need it, we've got it here."

The same can be said inside the Spartans' elaborate training facility, in which dozens of ailing players are soothed daily with rubdowns, ice, heat pads, whirlpools, and physical therapy. "There are bigger training rooms, but there are only so many ways you can invent the wheel," says Jeff Monroe, Michigan State University's coordinator of training. "We have all the equipment that is available to physical conditioning. Mr. Weaver has been an outstanding supporter of our program."

Weaver's dollars were well spent in the case of weak-side linebacker Kurt Larson, who snapped an Achilles tendon—usually a career-ending injury—in the spring of 1988. He missed just one game, and many credit MSU's

state-of-the-art medical facilities. "The best example of
how this facility has helped an athlete is Kurt Larson,"
Monroe says. "What it has done is provide day-to-day
management of an injury situation. We started rehabilita-
tion three days after he got out of the hospital. It's not
better than state-of-the-art, but I guess you can never be
better than that. But we're even with it."

On and on the chest-thumping continued through this
sensational 1988 summer of delight. Michigan State had
done it and done it within the rules, Perles reminded
anyone who would listen. And there were many who did.
The architect of the Stunt 4-3 defense was a hot com-
modity and drawing national attention. Even the Boston
Globe got into the act. In the paper's annual college
football preview issue, the *Globe* included an original—
and usually silly—fact about each head coach in their Top
20 selections by suggesting what to do "if he invited you
to dinner." The answer for Perles? "Order a beer for the
both of you." That drew a hearty chuckle from the man
who gained quite a reputation around East Lansing
nightspots as an assistant in the 1960s. "I don't even have
a beer a week anymore," Perles cracked.

This was the peak of the Perles era, and he beamed
with satisfaction from head to toe. At practice, he would
roam around the field, chatting with supporters, joking
with coaches. He'd blow his whistle to end practice and
take great pride in telling his players when breakfast
would be the next morning before sauntering into his
office, the evening sun dropping delicately behind the
Daugherty Building. The Disneyland ride hadn't stopped.
"The sun's shining, it's warm, it's a heck of a day," Perles
said after a particularly inspiring spring scrimmage. "I
think the interest is here between students, fans, people.
We've got a good reputation. We just had a coaches'
meeting, then we had a players' meeting, then we had a

practice. Nobody got hurt and the sun is shining. Heck of a day. It's beautiful."

But an unexpected dark cloud was about to dampen those spirits and the whole season. When superstar offensive lineman Tony Mandarich secretly applied for the National Football League draft, he put his amateur status and senior season in great jeopardy. The preseason Outland Trophy favorite was initially banned for the year by the National Collegiate Athletic Association, but the penalty was later reduced to three games. Still, the MSU coaches were saddled with the headache of reshuffling the offensive line before fall practice even began. The solution? Move veteran left guard Bob Kula into Mandarich's left tackle position, and fill Kula's slot with an unheralded sophomore, Eric Moten. "It's not like I was thinking about this while I was on vacation on the beaches of California, but I knew it was a possibility," quipped offensive line coach Pat Morris. "As a coach, you get prepared for any possibility."

Including injuries. The 1987 Big Ten champs were remarkably injury-free during their historic run. That same luck didn't carry over into 1988, as three returning starters from MSU's highly touted Gang Green defense missed the September 10 opener. Larson snapped a tendon during spring practice, while defensive end John Budde (knee) and safety Harlon Barnett (shin splints) were autumn casualties. This created havoc for an already-juggling defensive coaching staff, with hot-tempered Nick Saban having left for the Houston Oilers.

Yet, the afterglow from Pasadena overshadowed all the distractions. The veterans reported on August 19 wearing "Pound Green Pound" T-shirts, and some even dared to think a most devilish thought: *national championship.*

On that same day, though, the head man had his mind elsewhere. It is ironic that during the most satisfying 12 months of his coaching career, Perles was also choked by the pain of losing those around him. As the players shuffled into Perles' office to say hello, news came from Pittsburgh that long-time Steelers' owner Art Rooney, Sr. remained in critical condition after suffering a stroke. Perles' mentor Duffy Daugherty, as well as close friends Jack Breslin and Father Jerome MacEachin, had passed away recently, and now the 87-year-old Rooney lay bedridden. "He treated my kids like they were his own sons," Perles said slowly, looking off into the distance. "He was great to me and my family. This has been a tough time for me lately." George Perles' fiercest attribute, besides his frightening temper, is his loyalty to those who have helped his career and his family. Nothing matters more. A few days later, Rooney died, and Perles was crushed by the news. A red-faced and disoriented Perles, making last-minute plans to fly to Pittsburgh, could muster only one sorrowful statement: "I guess I'll see him tomorrow."

Although surrounded by gloom and uncertainty, no one really expected a letdown. "There's no complacency here," said senior safety John Miller. "George isn't going to let that happen. He's chewed us out and everything. We're going to keep working hard for all that Rutgers stuff coming up."

That "Rutgers stuff" turned out to be a bitter reminder to fans that 1987 was a lovely aberration, a joyful blip on the grand screen of college football. Michigan State came out flat-footed and nervous. Rutgers scored 17 second-quarter points and shocked the Spartans, 17-13. The Michigan State crowd, still recovering from Rose Bowl hangovers, left in disbelief. The Spartans' final effort to avoid embarrassment disappeared when tailback Blake Ezor, who had rushed for 196 yards, fumbled on the Scarlet Knights' ten-yard line with 5:23 remaining. The modest Rutgers attack then accentuated the defeat with three first downs to run out the clock. A Rutgers sign trumpeted, "The Roses are Dead." Indeed, they were, and a dozen slap-happy Rutgers administrators floated around the postgame press area like it was V-J Day. President Ed Broustein even hugged a reporter. "Ah, you came to write about the rinky-dinks," he said. But these "rinky-dinks" stared Big Ten tradition, the aura of the Rose Bowl win, and the previous year's Number 2 defense right in the face—and proceeded to stuff it right down MSU's throat. As quarterback Scott Erney tried to explain the win to a group of reporters, an administrator broke through to shake his hand. "Son, you've done a lot for Rutgers today," he said.

But not a whole lot for the Spartans, who were left to explain how a team thinking national title could lose to a perennial loser. A year later, Perles was still on the defensive. "How many have we blown?" he asked. "We usually don't lose games we should win. It's happened on a couple of occasions, that's all. And that was one of them."

The "rinky-dink" portion of the schedule was over, however. The next two teams—eventual national champion Notre Dame and Florida State—pounded Michigan State into a 0-3 hole. The Irish humiliated the previous season's Number 1 rushing defense with a perfectly executed option offense that riddled the Spartans for 245 yards on the ground and a 20-3 win. It was the first time since 1984 that Michigan State had allowed more than 200 rushing yards in a game. "The best feeling in the world is coming downfield and seeing four or five yards ahead of you with not a green jersey around," said Notre Dame's chief weapon, Mark Green, who totaled 125 yards. Meanwhile, the Spartans (13 rushing yards in the second half) were stuffed repeatedly by the Irish. When Mike Stonebreaker returned an interception 39 yards for a touchdown late in the fourth quarter, the defending Big Ten champs were reeling. "We're trying to hold the pieces together," Perles said.

Now, a defensive unit that was heralded from coast to coast one year earlier was beginning to be questioned. Was 1987 that much of a fluke? Had Saban been that important? It was obvious that the preseason injuries were taking a toll. "I'm not concerned with the defense," Miller said. "We have a lot of talent, and when Budde and Barnett get back, we'll be at full strength."

Perles, ever the kind loser, failed to draw the same correlation. "You'll never catch me saying that—we're not going to make any excuses," he insisted, although he would abandon that noble trait after Michigan State's 1989 loss to Michigan. "But there's no question that we're happy they're back. This is the healthiest we've been, without a doubt. It's not even close."

When Michigan State traveled to Tallahassee, Florida, to face the Seminoles, no one really gave the limping Spartans a chance. Basically, they didn't have one. Gang Green again was nonexistent as Florida State University waltzed to a 30-7 win. Although the Spartans rushed for 201 yards, they completed just one pass, a 25-yard touchdown strike to Andre Rison in the third quarter. That was it. The team returned to East Lansing a miserable 0-3, aware that the program had not fully evolved into a true national power as yet. For one thing, Michigan State lacked an imaginative offense, and McAllister was struggling horribly. If there was one ray of hope on that long flight home it was that the Big Ten conference schedule had not yet started. The conference of Woody and Bo was now a slumbering dinosaur in the new speed-oriented college game. MSU fit that formula perfectly.

There was another reason to be upbeat: the return of Mandarich, Budde, Larson, and Barnett to full-time duty. "We have no complaints, health-wise, now," Perles said. Still, it was painfully evident that the wonderment of 1987 would not be repeated, even with Michigan State at full strength. MSU hosted a sinking Iowa team to open the conference schedule, and treated the 76,348 fans—who braved a torrential rainstorm to watch the game—to a truly dull affair.

The game ended in an unsatisfying 10-10 tie. Both teams had chances to win the game in the final seconds, but both kickers failed on field goal attempts. The normally reliable John Langeloh missed his third field goal of the day, a 45-yarder with 16 seconds left in the game. "I thought it was good," Langeloh said. "I had my arms raised, thinking it might help." It didn't.

Then, after a 38-yard completion to Travis Watkins, the Hawkeyes had their opportunity to snatch a victory from the jaws of a tie. Jeff Skillet's 51-yard attempt at the gun, however, sailed just wide of the left upright. "I had already started celebrating," Skillet said. "I thought it was good."

Perhaps the lone thrill of the afternoon came because of Rison's outstanding 48-yard touchdown reception in the third quarter. After slipping on the wet turf, Rison caught the ball at the Iowa 30, eluded two tacklers, sprinted down the right sideline, and dragged two defenders—and the frustrations of an 0-3 start—across the goal line for six points. It was a great individual effort, which underlined the speedster's untapped potential at MSU. Though Rison left as the school's all-time leading receiver, fans still lament the fact that they never saw half the things he could do with a football. The potential All-American was lost behind a suffocating run-oriented offense, and he counted the days until the NFL draft. Rison was a sure thing in professional ball, which is one of the reasons he and Lansing agent Charles Tucker became particularly close during Rison's time at Michigan State.

Sandy Brown, who owns an Okemos sporting goods store called The Athlete Connection, has had significant business problems with Rison's agent. She said Rison

would come in, pick out expensive shoes or other merchandise, and charge the amount to a tab Tucker was
keeping at the store. Brown complains that the tab, which
has become as high as $10,000, has never been paid.
Tucker called her a "witch," she says, and has refused to
pay. "I'm scared of him," she says. "He thinks he can do
whatever he wants."

Rison isn't the first Michigan State receiver to break
NCAA violations by accepting illegal payments while still
in school. Mark Ingram, first-round pick of the New York
Giants in 1987, was one of 43 players involved with
super-agent Norby Walters, who later was indicted for
coercing players into signing contracts.

Besides his taste for expensive shoes, Rison also had
a knack for predicting the future, especially where he and
his buddy McAllister were concerned. The two would
spend many nights together just talking, whether the
subject happened to be women, the media, or each other's
place in MSU football history. Early in their relationship,
Rison, ever the dreamer, told McAllister the team
wouldn't reach the Rose Bowl until McAllister was
quarterback. Rison also said the two of them would hook
up for a bomb and a key play in the big game. All three
predictions came true. "He said that we were going to
come from nowhere to have one of the best connections
in the country," McAllister said. "And I'll be known as one
of the top quarterbacks in the country."

Through four games of 1988, that simply didn't happen. McAllister completed just 28 of 64 passes (43
percent), miserably misfiring many of them. The offense
contributed only three touchdowns through four games,
and the fans would let the quiet leader know about it
every time he stepped on the field. Against Iowa, the
"boos" hit a frightening crescendo, drawing sympathy
from Perles. "I don't want to criticize anybody in public,"
Perles said. "This isn't pro football. There's only one guy

whom McAllister has to be concerned with, and that's
George. That's the only guy he has to have hang with him,
no matter what the fan reaction is." The fans' reaction
was, simply, this: replace the quarterback who, ten
months earlier, had delivered a Rose Bowl title. Replace
him now.

◆ ◆ ◆

Bobby McAllister never wanted to be a hero.

Such lofty personal goals always seemed
presumptuous to him. He just wanted respect and
privacy, and he never grasped the fact that the position
he played made both these luxuries long shots at best.
McAllister, who knew how to pass, but not always when
and where, came from Pompano Beach, Florida to have a
look at big-time Midwestern football. Eventually, he
covered his eyes. It wasn't that he didn't enjoy Michigan
State University; he did. But what was this strange fixation
people seemed to have with "Bobby bashing?" If he ran the
football, fans and members of the news media called on
him to stay in the pocket. If he stayed home and was
sacked, they wondered aloud why he hadn't mobilized.

"It's just hard keeping people happy," said McAllister
during a private moment in 1988. By this time, he had
made it a practice not to speak with certain reporters,
mainly because he had nothing good to say to them. That
made the moments he did talk seem special, as though he
were speaking to a friend. "First, they want you to win,
and when you do, they find something else they don't like.
I guess they think we don't pass enough, so we're not
exciting. Well, I always thought winning was exciting. I
guess I was wrong."

McAllister's bitterness can most likely be traced to his
freshman year, 1985, when he was forced into action
because of a thumb injury to starter Dave Yarema. In that
season, the Spartans suffered under their young leader,

losing 27-10 at Notre Dame and escaping with a 7-3 win over Western Michigan in what might have been the most boring athletic competition in history. Even when Mc-Allister threw for 275 yards in a near-upset of Number 1 Iowa, the prevailing feeling was that he didn't belong. When Yarema returned to win six straight games and send MSU to the All-American Bowl, that feeling grew stronger than ever.

McAllister eventually began cutting out negative articles about his play and scribbling *"F—- 'em"* on them with a magic marker. It was a way to relieve the frustration.

"The media are just writing what they think the fans want to hear," McAllister said from his Pompano Beach home during an interview in January 1990. He is now on the roster of the Canadian Football League's Toronto Argonauts, and hopes to have an NFL shot someday. "The fans, well, they're paying their money, so I guess they can think what they want."

Of all the possible reasons for McAllister's lack of acceptance in East Lansing, one sticks out as the most disturbing, if true: He is one of only two black quarterbacks in the history of the school. Says Pat Shurmur, "Whenever you have a black quarterback, that is going to be a problem for some stupid people."

"I didn't really give it much thought," says McAllister, "but it's a dilemma that goes on all around the country. It's not the color of a person's skin that matters. I mean, is that person winning ball games? That's the most important thing. It's starting to become an accepted happening all over the country now. You see a lot of black quarterbacks in Bowl games . . . but I hate to even say the word 'black,' because color doesn't matter. It's not a statistic, like wins or losses."

Yarema agrees, but acknowledges that some see it differently. "I've heard people talking about it, saying,

'Black guys aren't quarterbacks'; 'They're not smart enough'; 'They can't do it.' Bobby is as smart as anyone I've been here with."

He is also one of the most successful, if Michigan State's first Rose Bowl triumph since 1956 is any barometer. When the 1987 team lacked an offensive identity, McAllister grabbed the football and created one. If leadership is finding solutions to serious problems, then was he not a leader?

"We came together as a team that year," he says. "It just showed I was capable of leading the team. The defense gave us great field position, and we could feel the electricity when things were going well. We felt it was time for us to come together and let our God-given talent come out."

But McAllister's contentment, just like a football fan's patience, never seemed to last too long. After he talked glowingly about throwing early and often in 1988, the vision caved in with the Spartans' 0-4-1 start. Some costly interceptions and questionable decisions from the quarterback position prompted Spartan followers to look toward sophomore Dan Enos for help. For McAllister, it seemed like his freshman year all over again, when fans had waited desperately for Yarema to save the day.

"Bobby felt bad," says Derrick Reed, a Spartan cornerback who was close to McAllister that season. "He felt disappointed, because who wouldn't be? He kept trying to reason that the fans and the media don't understand football, and that what he was going through was part of being a quarterback."

No matter how hard he tried, McAllister failed to link his boyhood images of football glory with the miserable game he was playing now. Somewhere along the line, it stopped being fun, and McAllister might have given it up, if not for the genuine and much-needed support of his teammates. "We were behind him," says Ezor, who has always defended McAllister, even when it hasn't been easy to do so. "Hey, he was our quarterback. We said to him, 'Don't listen to anybody. Just keep your head straight,' and then we would surround him in the huddle and shield out everything. It didn't seem right that all our losing and everything came down on him."

No, it didn't seem right. But maturity has taught McAllister to grab onto any silver lining he finds and squeeze it tightly. He also relished the fact that his teammates never turned on him, that they raised eyebrows at the criticism and dismissed it as the senseless babble of an uninformed minority. All McAllister ever wanted to be, after all, was a single part of a very impressive team, one component of a legacy. He did that, and now he will continue to play in the Canadian Football League, richer because of the experience.

"I have no regrets," he says, and it sounds as if he means it.

◆ ◆ ◆

The misery for McAllister and the Spartans didn't end in Ann Arbor the following week. Not many 0-3-1 teams find refuge at Michigan, and this week was no different. Once again, the MSU offense struggled. McAllister completed just 6 of 12 passes for 71 yards, and the Michigan defense held Michigan State to just two yards a carry. Still, the Spartans stayed within striking distance at 10-0 when Miller, the MSU hero in last year's intrastate game, intercepted a Michael Taylor pass and returned it to the Wolverine five-yard line early in the third quarter. Three runs had pushed the ball to the one, where Michigan State faced a fourth-and-goal decision. Perles played it safe, sending in Langeloh to boot an 18-yarder and make it 10-3. The anemic Spartans, however, never threatened again.

Punter Mike Gillette's 40-yard touchdown run on a fake punt sealed the Spartans' fate: a 17-3 loss and an

0-4-1 start. Moments before the fake, the Wolverine-killer Miller had blocked Gillette's punt, and Spartan Corey Pryor scooped up the ball and ran for an apparent game-tying touchdown. But winless teams aren't usually rewarded with such breaks. Freshman Alan Haller was called for jumping offsides, nullifying the score. "We were beaten by a better team out there today," MSU's 0-4-1 coach said in a dramatic understatement.

If the Spartans had resided in one of the nation's best conferences, the prospects for postseason play would be empty. Even in the floundering Big Ten, the Bowl chances for an 0-4-1 team were dim. But MSU knew if it could sweep its last six games—the only noteworthy opponent being Indiana University on November 12—perhaps some Bowl would be sympathetic toward their difficult preconference schedule, the suspension of Mandarich, and a team with three potential first-round draft picks (Mandarich, Rison, and junior linebacker Percy Snow).

So with George Perles imploring the obvious—"take them one game at a time"—the Spartans embarked on this voyage through the Big Ten's underworld. What better way to start a six-game winning streak than against woeful Northwestern, at Spartan Stadium? All the frustration and disappointment of 1988 was dumped squarely on Northwestern quarterback Greg Bradshaw during a 36-3 whipping of the Wildcats. Bradshaw appeared in the postgame interview room dazed and glassy-eyed, struggling to bend his knees to sit down in a wooden chair. The Spartan defense had been that punishing. "I'm going to be sore for a while," said Bradshaw, icing his swollen lip. "I've never felt this bad before. They were a very, very physical team. Every tackle was around the neck. They were tackling toward the head. Maybe it didn't happen as much as I think, but it just seemed they were always up around the head. Almost every pass play, I was getting rocked."

The mission traveled to Champaign, Illinois, and could easily have been named a country music hit, "The Revenge of Bobby the Kid." Michigan State erased an early 14-0 deficit to beat Illinois, 28-21. In addition to raising the season record to 2-4-1, Perles' favorite sight had to be the resurrection of quarterback Bobby McAllister, who threw for two touchdown passes and didn't throw an interception. Around friends and family, McAllister probably revelled in the return of his 1987 magic. But McAllister couldn't force a smile in front of members of the media, who had blamed the senior endlessly for the Spartans' poor start. The accurate and fleet McAllister, who can peg receivers with his shotgun-arm one play and scramble for a first down the next, showed up at Memorial Stadium. The charismatic and forgiving McAllister didn't. "We're not making the mistakes we did in the past," he said sternly. "It's kind of a relief because you know the talent is there when you score a lot of points. We have a lot of talent." There was McAllister, sitting uneasily in his chair, glaring at the folks taking notes. Every word was calculated, every thought restrained. There was no joy in his voice, and the bitterness over the way he had been treated spilled out. "This is just a different year; I can't dwell on that. Every year is different." That said, he stood up and left the room, his job done.

The road to 6-4-1 wouldn't be squeaky-clean. After Michigan State's 20-10 pounding of Ohio State the following week, rumors began to circulate that members of MSU's herculean offensive line were using steroids. Michigan State had buried the Buckeyes with 381 rushing yards—172 from sophomore Hyland Hickson and 155 from Blake Ezor—but the news afterwards was coming from the Buckeye dressing room, where OSU defensive lineman Greg Zackeroff claimed that the massive yardage total was the result of widespread steroid use. "We've always had a clean program—we do things the natural way," said Zackeroff, who questioned how a dozen Michigan State linemen were each able to lift more than 500 pounds. "I don't think anyone could spend more time in the weight room than [OSU linebacker] Chris Spielman. And he never benched more than 420 or 430." Perles dismissed the charges as poor sportsmanship, but it marked the first time opposing teams would say publicly what had been suspected in private since 1985.

As it turned out, the ground game—steroid-induced or not—was just getting started. Michigan State rushed the ball 68 times for 460 yards at Purdue, burying the Boilermakers 48-3. McAllister, who rushed for 94 yards, threw the ball just six times in a devastating display of smashmouth football. Ezor led the team with 150 yards and two touchdowns, but the spotlight was stolen by Kurt Larson, who picked off two Purdue passes and returned one 36 yards for a touchdown. The game meant the senior from Waukesha, Wisconsin had come full circle from that day in April when doctors had predicted that his playing days were over.

Larson had spent all summer rehabilitating his torn Achilles tendon, jumping forward in small, rabbit-like leaps on the sidelines, watching his teammates prepare for the season. The bunny hops worked; the senior co-captain had recovered, and so had the 4-4-1 Spartans. Both were in familiar form. "I don't want to start looking back until the season is over," Larson said. "I'm satisfied with the way I've come back from the injury, but we have two games left."

Neither of these remaining games was much of a contest. At Indiana, Michigan State again dominated on the ground, rushing for 376 yards in a 38-12 thumping. The stage belonged to Ezor, who scored three touchdowns on 250 yards. All the pregame talk centered around Indiana's fine tailback Anthony Thompson, but the Spartan defense held the Heisman candidate to only 34 yards. It was Ezor

who turned heads. "I was really fired up," the junior
tailback said. "I wanted to prove that I was a good back,
too."

Meanwhile, the 5-4-1 Spartans were becoming an at-
tractive alternative for the lesser Bowls, and Perles was
doing an effective job of campaigning. "Do I think we
deserve a Bowl bid? Yes."

Perles wouldn't have to wait too long. The word came
on Monday that the Gator Bowl would offer Michigan State
the bid if it beat lowly Wisconsin at home. Perles tried to
prevent a news leak, but when word escaped that the
Spartans would be going to their fourth Bowl game in five
years, the coach used his weekly news conference to
blister the media and their use of unidentified sources.
"When you use an unidentified source, you incriminate
hundreds," Perles raged. "If someone here can explain
how much courage it takes to do that, I'm willing to listen."
The lecture was understandable; it was an emotional,
knee-jerk reaction. Now that he was so close to a Bowl
prize that one month earlier had seemed like a fairy tale,
Perles did not want overconfidence seeping into his
players.

It didn't. Ezor added another three touchdowns to his
season slate, giving him nine, and Langeloh booted five
field goals in a 36-0 win over the Badgers. The
Spartans had completed an improbable six-game run
to the Gator Bowl, and George Perles savored every
minute of it: "I wanted to go to the Gator Bowl so bad, I
could taste it."

Aside from the jubilation, there were signs that the
madness of collegiate athletics in East Lansing was beginning to spin out of control. After the Wisconsin game,
thousands of fans poured onto the field, tearing down the
goalpost that stood next to the players' tunnel. Then this
seemingly harmless celebration of a second-place finish
turned tragic. A security officer was rushed away in

serious condition after being accosted by several students. While George Perles delivered his famous
oratory—"If anybody says anything bad about the Gator
Bowl, I'm going to punch them in the nose"—dozens of
trampled fans, mostly women, were being dragged into the
tunnel, most of them bruised, and some bloodied.

Meanwhile, the Badger players struggled to explain
their horrible 1-10 season. Here was Todd Nelson,
Wisconsin's senior captain, red-faced and holding back
tears. The light from the television cameras shined bright-
ly in his face, and his thoughts were choppy, each word
carrying with it a sorrowful chunk of broken pride. "It was
tough, very tough, being captain of this football team," he
said softly, slowly. "I don't know what to say to the
younger guys. What could I say? It was just miserable."
One wonders just how much "character" had been cul-
tivated there.

The Spartans didn't have time to feel sorry for Nelson
or anybody else. They had completed a remarkable run
through the Big Ten, and the fact that most of the wins
had come against league "doormats" didn't quite matter.
And why should it? Perles and his team walked into
Lansing's Clarion Hotel for their annual postseason banquet with a great deal of pride. The record 0-4-1 became
a symbol of George Perles' so-called family working
together, and he would have gold 0-4-1 pins made for each
player. They had been through war—with the fans, the
news media, and, to a certain extent, with themselves. And
they had won.

Ironically, the Gator Bowl against Georgia highlighted
the fact that both McAllister and Rison were leaving MSU
with much of their talent untapped. McAllister threw for
288 yards and three touchdowns, all to his best friend
Rison. Trailing 24-7, McAllister and Rison led a furious,
pass-happy, acrobatic comeback that fell just short, 34-
27.

Still, the loss didn't taint Michigan State's recovery from oblivion. Perles, as he had always promised, indeed turned a negative into a positive. His philosophy worked, which was fortunate, because the next two years saw it tested again. And again.

8

1989: NEW AGE, OLD PROBLEM

"Let me tell you something: When you get that ball, you've got a second to think, 'Am I going over the top or am I going to try to find a hole?' There was nothing to jump over."

– Blake Ezor

The doubts that became part of a transitional football season at Michigan State neither involved nor affected Percy Snow. MSU's senior middle linebacker, perhaps the finest collegiate football player in the country in 1989, was to become the seventh Perles protégé in as many years to be selected in the NFL draft's opening round. That much was certain.

"I don't go out on the field worrying about anyone," said Snow, as he stalked about Spartan Stadium during the school's picture day in the heat of August. "I'll put anybody on their butt. If they can't take it, they know what they can do. I won't show pity for anyone. You could put my brother or sister out there at midfield, and I'd give them my best shot."

Snow doesn't smile after saying such things; he doesn't smile much at all. Here and there, he'll muster an embarrassed smile to a reporter, but never a football smile. Snow, quite simply, was never taught that football and joviality should go together. At times his violent challenges sound pretentious or even childish, but who's going to tell him? The plain truth is that Snow's pretense alone can make a defense sing.

So how could things go wrong for the Spartans, with this tower of strength as a leader?

Snow's emblematic ferocity, after all, was fostered in the roughest section of Canton, Ohio—where football dreams rise with the sun. He came to Michigan State because they promised him he could start at middle linebacker as a sophomore, after Shane Bullough fulfilled his eligibility. "Everybody wanted Percy," George Perles says. "That was a heck of a recruiting job." But Snow could have started as a freshman; he refused to be red-shirted, and Perles obliged out of fear that his prize might transfer. As a special team catalyst during the 1986 season, Snow made five tackles against Western Michigan in just 13 minutes of play.

"I think you can teach kids to hit," says Thom Mc-Daniels, who coached Snow at Canton McKinley High School. "But you can't teach kids to love to hit. Percy loves to hit."

Snow was on the path to stardom. He was proclaimed anchor of the Stunt 4-3 in 1987, earning Rose Bowl MVP honors for his 17-tackle performance, and is now the second leading tackler in Michigan State University history.

Yet, with all this in their favor, the 1989 Spartans still managed only a 7-4 record and a jaded junket to the Aloha Bowl. Defense, again, was not the factor that prevented

MSU from defeating top national schools and thus lifting itself to their level of respectability. It was the offense, which was expected to improve with junior Dan Enos accepting the tattered reins from Bobby McAllister. The same old concerns that had temporarily been washed away by a Rose Bowl championship resurfaced again when the Spartans won only two of their first six games in 1989. Not only did Perles' team not throw the ball enough, it seemed to lack the diversification to throw it well. Often, the patterns looked too similar, too simple, and matters of strategic sophistication are only answerable by coaches.

Morris Watts was named offensive coordinator by Perles in March 1986, after assistant coach Ted Guthard left to pursue private business interests. During his 24 years of coaching, Watts had directed quarterbacks for the USFL's Birmingham Stallions and Louisiana State University, and had also served as Indiana University's offensive coordinator from 1972 to 1983. But since arriving at MSU, he has been an offensive coach primarily on the defensive. Watts sat in his office two months before the 1989 season and talked of turning around MSU's image as a ground-oriented team. And he spoke with conviction. Whatever coaching magic this man possesses, it has not significantly affected the state of Spartan football affairs, and that hurts him. He spoke on this day like a man who was tired of having his name dragged through the mud.

"Sometimes it's not easy," said Watts. "We hear the boos. We know what's going on. But I think it's hard to coach if you don't have the courage to stick with your convictions." Still, Watts insisted the Spartans would throw more, and that Enos' ability to stay in the pocket would insure greater air support. He spoke regrettably about how McAllister's erratic arm and sometimes questionable judgment had made the Spartan coaches fearful of running intricate pass plays. A few weeks later, tailback

Blake Ezor reiterated that point by saying, "The reason we ran so much the last two years is because the coaches just weren't confident with Bobby."

But Enos was far from a savior, and MSU still was a program that experienced problems when chasing a talented team late in the game. After a humorous home-opening 49-0 rout of Miami of Ohio, the Spartans found themselves in close battles with national powers Notre Dame and Miami of Florida. Rose Bowl possibilities would not be damaged by losses to these schools—who at year's end would both claim to be national champion—but Perles felt ready to take an idealogical leap into the world of multifaceted super programs, which he felt was the next logical step.

But defense was still the only facet that was getting the Spartans by. In a 21-13 loss at Notre Dame, they shut down Irish quarterback Tony Rice's freewheeling option tendencies, but couldn't move the ball with the game on the line. On the game's final play, back-up quarterback John Gieselman was brought in cold to throw a Hail Mary prayer downfield, the rationale being that Enos couldn't throw it that far. Gieselman was no help either; he fumbled the snap.

Things were just as close at home against Miami, but also just as frustrating. Enos, who was kept on the run all afternoon by the Hurricanes' NFL-type defensive line, delivered a huge rushing touchdown, but MSU seemed confused later in what became a pass-or-die affair. Safety Harlon Barnett had tied the score at 20-20 with an interception return for a touchdown, but two Miami field goals put the Spartans in a 26-20 bind late in the fourth quarter. An upset that was tangible would require a sophisticated two-minute drill against a gifted secondary. And so MSU lost.

Perles and his Spartans got a break, though, when the Big Ten schedule opened in Iowa City. Hawkeye Coach

Hayden Fry had lived through three ties during a forget-table 1988 season, and seemed determined never again to leave a football game undecided. Trailing 17-14 with less than a minute to play, Iowa went for broke on fourth-and-ten from the Spartan ten-yard line and was buried by the MSU defense. "I never gave a second thought to taking a field goal," said Fry, whom Perles has referred to as "that guy in the cornfield." "We were out to win that football game."

Enos had completed 20 of 25 passes for 217 yards and sophomore Courtney Hawkins was becoming his favorite target. Sophomore tailback Tico Duckett also sprang on the scene, rushing for 275 yards. But Iowa was not the powerful, confident team it been so often in the past. It was young. It was vulnerable. And the Spartans knew their true Pasadena test would come the next week against Michigan.

An almost balmy October afternoon created a carnival atmosphere when the two teams met in East Lansing to settle long-standing differences. But one of the largest tailgate mobs ever assembled at Michigan State was dis-appointed with both the quality of play and the outcome. The Spartans, who passed for 214 yards but only ran for 77, trailed 10-0 at halftime and concentrated much of their energy on one fateful third-quarter drive. They began the odyssey on their own 21 with 6:35 left in the quarter, and relied heavily on Ezor to move the ball downfield, which he did with surprising success. A reception by Hawkins moved the Spartans into Wolverine territory, and Ezor's innovation after that seemed to guarantee the first MSU score. But things got interesting when Ezor was stopped at the Michigan three-yard line on a second down. His subsequent attempt to burrow through a wall of hate earned him two yards on third down, setting up a roman-tic struggle between two football programs fighting for intrastate prominence: fourth-and-goal at the one-yard line.

A field goal would have made the score 10-3 with plenty of time to play, and indeed that would have been the predictable decision from the ever-conservative Perles. But the drama here was too perfect, the possibility of demoralizing Michigan too great. It could be that, in what became the pivotal moment of the 1989 season, Perles let his heated jealousy of Michigan Coach Bo Schembechler stand in the way of cool and rational thinking. "There was no debate," he said after the game. "That's a good play for us, but Michigan got great penetration."

Great enough, in fact, for Ezor to doubt his chances to dive over the pile for a score. Fullback Steve Mongomery, Ezor's main blocker, had been knocked out of the play, so Ezor lowered his head and tried to find an opening at ground level. When he ran into linebacker J.J. Grant and safety Tripp Welborne, MSU had once again failed to make the big play. And Ezor received much of the blame for the eventual 10-7 loss.

"I've already forgotten about it," Ezor said tersely when reminded of the play the following January. "[The media] wants to assume that that would be the big play to remember. I laugh at that. There were too many big plays in that game. It's all bullshit. Let me tell you something: When you get that ball, you've got a split second to think, 'Am I going to go over the top or am I going to try to find a hole?' There was nothing to jump over."

Ezor met Grant at the Japan Bowl in early January, and tried to set his own mind at ease by asking the opinion of someone who had been involved. "I'm sick of hearing it from other people," he said to Grant. "You were the linebacker, and you were right there. If I had jumped, would I have made it?"

"I took on that block so well that I knocked him down," was Grant's reply. "If you were going to jump, you would have had to jump pretty high."

That soothed Ezor somewhat, but the abuse he absorbed after the Michigan loss intensified a long-building distaste for East Lansing. For all his breathless bravado, at times Ezor simply came off as a kid who was too far from home.

♦ ♦ ♦

Ezor carried with him some big-league credentials when he sauntered onto the MSU campus in August 1985, but nobody was overly impressed. Sure, this was a kid who had been recruited by Notre Dame, Miami of Florida, and Penn State, this was a *Parade* All-American, a guy who scored 35 touchdowns at Las Vegas' Bishop Gorman High School and ran the 100 meters in under 11 seconds. "I think he's probably the fastest white kid in existence," said Chuck Gerber, who coached Ezor and his three brothers at Gorman. Ezor was five-feet-ten and less than 180 pounds, but despite these physical limitations, he thought himself very cool. Very *it*. There must have been some mistake. Was this curly blond Casino Casinova really going to spend the next four years of his life in East Lansing? It was almost laughable.

"It was really obvious he wasn't from around here," recalls Brad Reaume, who became Ezor's roommate halfway through that year and remained so for five years. "I mean, he was wearing gold. People from out West dress differently, they talk differently. He just didn't like Michigan very much." Said Montgomery: "He definitely was a fast talker."

But Ezor couldn't talk his way out of a red-shirt that 1985 season. And in 1986, he ran into both mononucleosis and star-studded tailback Lorenzo White, who was making an all-out lunge for the Heisman

Trophy. After six games, Ezor had overcome the mono, but battling the White mystique was a whole different story. When he met with Perles to complain about his secondary status, he learned a quick lesson about public relations. And he learned how much Perles wanted a Heisman in the building.

"Lorenzo was up for the Heisman, and I wasn't," said Ezor, who gained just 337 yards in 1986. "I just had to accept that. I mean, what was I going to do? Sure, a lot of publicity problems had to do with Lorenzo. There was always an obstacle the media was putting in front of me. If it wasn't Lorenzo, it was something else."

The Ezor–White rivalry—some called it a tandem or a duo, but it was a rivalry—finally reached its zenith in 1987. White was once again a leading Heisman candidate, but people couldn't fail to notice Ezor, the small blur who was taking minutes and yardage away from the supposed star of the show. It was an odd coupling of running style, to say the least. Where White would cut, Ezor would crash. Where the nimbler, swifter cover boy would play with defenders, Ezor would play with fire, hurling himself directly into the line. And he got there so fast, the yards began to add up.

"Everybody would say, 'How can you run right into those big guys? Avoid them,'" Ezor said. "But I've always run right at people. My body's used to it. I don't know, maybe I can endure more than other people."

Perhaps physically, but Ezor's pride found White's media brigade tougher to endure. He outgained a healthy White from a substitute role in three games, rushed for 617 total yards, averaged more per carry than his nemesis, and still fought tooth and nail for something all the gold or nice clothes or fast-talking in the world couldn't bring him: respect. "Blake is just so conscious of everything going on around him—who's getting the credit, who's getting the publicity," said Montgomery. "I think a lot of that stems from his being from Las Vegas, because there's just so much going on there. You have to be able to keep track of everything."

Whatever it was—perhaps the bitterness left over from 1987 or the realization that the backfield spotlight was completely his—something motivated Ezor to gain 1,496 yards in 1988. No Spartan runner except White had ever gained more. Actually, the motivation behind this feat may have evolved from a meaningless game against Northwestern in the season's sixth week. For a guy so aware of statistics and publicity, Northwestern is the biggest game of the year. It was a possible 300-yard afternoon, and it was Homecoming, but Ezor dislocated his elbow in the second quarter and gained only 68 yards. "I just fell on the arm wrong," he says. "It was a fluke thing. I took two aspirin and said, 'Put me back in.'" But Perles didn't—not during such a Tupperware party. So Ezor watched freshman Scott Selzer and sophomore Hyland Hickson combine for 213 yards in the 36-3 laugher. Blake actually felt five-foot-ten, or smaller.

The injury threatened more than his health; it threatened his job. Ezor averaged 146 yards a game for the rest of the season—including a 250-yard day at Indiana—and never, ever let it be known again that he was hurt. "He took lumps in every game he played," Montgomery said. "He'd be in the shower and it would look like he had tattoos all over his body. The kid's got a threshold of pain like you wouldn't believe."

Ezor wasn't able to ignore a separated sternum he suffered in the second game of 1989 against Notre Dame. He missed two games because of it. But his desire to be mentioned in the same breath with White was powerful, and he even managed to forget about his goal-line failure against Michigan. By the end of the season, Ezor had become the first MSU running back in history to gain 1,000 yards in consecutive seasons.

"Usually, running backs like a vacation on the first couple days of the week because they worked so hard on Saturday, but Blake was different," Perles said. "He wanted to show he was ready every day. And he was."

◆ ◆ ◆

Perles, though, wasn't ready to accept the Spartans' defeat against Michigan as he usually believes it is respectable to do. One of his favorite adages—and there are literally thousands—is, "Make no excuses after you lose." But some of Schembechler's statements after the game infuriated Perles to the point of vengeance. "The best team won," was probably the comment that pierced Perles' heart, mainly because he firmly believed it wasn't true.

The win must have been especially sweet for Schembechler, who may have known at the time that he was on his farewell tour through the Big Ten. When Schembechler stepped down in December, he probably felt especially satisfied that he had squelched Perles' challenge of state supremacy so convincingly. Of the seven meetings between the two, Schembechler had won five, and most in dominating fashion. The combined final tally of their battles reads: *SCHEMBECHLER 145, PERLES 52.*

That aching reality was evident at Perles' press conference two days after the game, as he arrived equipped with a videotape machine to show the media how the Spartans had been robbed. He pointed out how the Wolverines' snapper had rocked the football before a missed Michigan field goal in the second quarter, and how this had caused MSU defender Todd Murray to jump offside. When Michigan kicker J.D. Carlson was successful with his second attempt, it became the winning margin. The picture didn't explain all of MSU's blunders in the second half, but perhaps it relieved some of Perles' anger toward his intrastate nemesis. Of Schembechler's

postgame comments, Perles muttered, "nice humble statement," and his bitter sarcasm rang through the room.

Things couldn't possibly get worse in Spartanland—
until the next Saturday. With the Spartans leading Illinois
10-7 and with 1:36 remaining in the cold, dreary affair,
junior tailback Hyland Hickson made the game, and the
season, colder and drearier than anyone thought possible.
He fumbled the ball at his own 35, and Jeff George's
touchdown pass to Mike Bellamy 30 seconds later gave
the Illini a rather generous 14-10 victory. Suddenly, the
Spartans were 2-4 and glancing at the "Future Schedules"
portion of the media guide.

Except, of course, for Snow. He was finally receiving
the national acclaim he had always deserved, and that was
almost as enjoyable for the senior as hurting people on
the football field. His back-breaking tenacity down the
stretch—in which the Spartans downed Purdue, Indiana,
Minnesota, Northwestern, and Wisconsin—enabled him
to capture both the Butkus and the Lombardi awards, the
former for linebackers and the latter for both linebackers
and linemen. In so doing, he became the first Spartan ever
to win even one of the four major awards—the Heisman,
the Outland, the Lombardi, and the Butkus.

"The days go by quickly," he said late in the season,
sitting restlessly in the Daugherty Building and reminisc-
ing. "It seems like I just started playing here yesterday. I
guess when you're having fun, time flies. And now it's time
to move on."

The 7-4 Spartans, as it turned out, moved five time
zones to the west to play the University of Hawaii in the
Aloha Bowl. The game was played on Christmas Day, and
the gifts were everywhere. The smallish and overeager
Rainbows fumbled the ball early and often against Snow
and the MSU defense, losing a laugher, 33-13.

A highly motivated Ezor led the charge on the offense,
scoring three touchdowns. When he scored his first, he

waved a humiliating finger in the face of a helpless Hawaii defender, which prompted viewers once again to call him a braggart, a brat, or worse.

But Ezor had been similarly taunted from the moment he arrived on the island, mostly by the Hawaii team. "They were at war with us, especially with me," he says. "They never intended to make friends. They just had this attitude. We went to work out one day and there were signs all over the weight room, pictures of me with 'Convict Comes to Hawaii' written next to it. I mean, they made this big deal about it, and that really pissed me off when I saw it. I paid my dues for that. I'm sick of people throwing it in my face."

The abuse continued when Ezor and some of his teammates entered a Honolulu bar on the second night of their stay. "The guys from the Hawaii team were there, and they started calling me 'convict' and 'jailbird.' We started getting into it. We scuffled, but there were no punches thrown. They kicked me out because there were all locals there, and I just stayed inside the rest of the time and decided that I'd get them back on game day. So when it came time to play and I did all that taunting and hot-dogging—whatever you want to call it—it was specifically for one reason: They made me do it."

Ezor was happy to do it, putting some odd finishing touches, fittingly, on what had been a rather odd season. But the problems and intrigue were still brewing in East Lansing.

EPILOGUE

Michigan State University Football Coach George Perles' initial reaction to concerns that his program was beginning to take a negative toll on the university—through the steroid scandal, his questionable ascension to athletic director, and the lawless behavior of some of his players—was typical. It is the way he has handled every controversy that threatens to rock his ship: with a bland statement that doesn't really mean anything, but sounds good to the casual observer. "I've always said our priorities are family, education, and then football," Perles said at the beginning of the team's 1990 spring practice. "We'll move football down to Number 4 and are always looking for ways to move it down to Number 5 or 6 and still have a chance for the Rose Bowl. We'll move health to Number 1 . . . I'll make a positive out of this if it's the last thing I do."

George Perles' set of "priorities" is continually offered to quiet critics, but this papier maché collection of phrases crumbles against reality.

185

Instead of pouring out glittering generalities, what is needed is a set of specific guidelines to better govern the program. Because Michigan State and other major college programs have been slow to react to widespread problems, steps have been taken by higher administrative forces to ameliorate the situation. These steps include:

- Random drug testing, a more direct and effective procedure to police a program, will be required by colleges during the 1990 season.
- At its 1991 convention, the NCAA Presidents' Commission will sponsor a proposal limiting college athletes to 20 hours a week in their sport, an average reduction of about 33 percent. The commission also will ask that athletes receive one day off a week during the season.

Though these reforms are a step in the right direction, there still is a great distance to travel. Some suggestions for improvement:

- Hire a full-time career counselor to make student-athletes aware of the many academic avenues available to them. If Greg Croxton spends so much of his time simply keeping players eligible, perhaps he needs help fulfilling other facets of his job.
- Allow athletes a one-year extension of their scholarship upon completion of their eligibility. This grace period would give serious students the time to graduate without football interfering.
- Institute a mandatory one-game suspension for players charged with a misdemeanor or more serious offense. Although a person is innocent until proven guilty, this would serve as a deterrent to weed out the casual offender. And, after all, what is one football game?
- Seriously investigate past dealings between the football program, student-athletes and professors. Michigan State's reform committee, SPARC, does

not plan to look at the past in making its recom-
mendations for the future, but it should. It would
be wise to learn from the past so the same sins
aren't repeated.

Currently, the Michigan State University football program appears to be spinning out of control. In the end,
one is left wondering whether anything has been learned
from the excesses and errors of the past four years.
Perhaps more important is the question of where MSU is
headed in the 1990s. One thing is certain, however:
George Perles will never escape the negative impact of his
program and policies.

You have already read Perles' declarations about
academics and integrity being treasured, while wins and
bowl appearances are simply a side dish on the Duffy
Daugherty Football Building training table. Former Spartan players—the stars and scrubs alike—tell a different
story, a sad tale of a professional organization shrewdly
manipulating the nuisance of eligibility to achieve one
sweet goal: a New Year's Day trip to Pasadena. That is fact.
Ask Blake Ezor. He made football history at Michigan
State, and nothing—be it an ornery Ohio State linebacker
or the poor timing of finals week—stood in his way. As of
this writing, Ezor is still without a degree, facing yet more
legal trouble in a town to which he never quite became
acclimated. No one really cares, though. His last moment
in a Spartan uniform was a great one. *That's* what matters.

One need look no farther than the first six months of
1990 for proof that the facade still exists. To soften the
controversy surrounding his appointment as athletic
director, Perles sought an old friend, his trusty cliché
machine, to soothe both alumni and members of the
media. Perles assured everyone MSU had priorities, and
that the university cared what happened to kids on and
off the field. He attributed the steroids saga ito the evil
creation of slanted reporting. "We've tested and retested

[for steroids]," Perles insisted. "We're at the top of the Big
Ten in that area." Michigan State's alumni sat back,
circled the September 22 home opener against Notre
Dame on their calendars, and smiled. There was joy in
East Lansing again.

Two months later, George Perles' feel-good festival
crashed to the ground when the Detroit *News* reported
something not included in his oratory—the facts. It seems
the only category in which Michigan State leads the Big
Ten is in positive steroid results. In more than four years
of "probable cause" drug testing, Michigan State conducted a total of 105 tests in the entire athletic department, including 41 for steroids. During that same time,
Ohio State University tested its athletes 1,911 times.
Michigan State had not, in fact, led the way in exposing
harmful and dangerous behavior among its athletes. That,
we know, is simply not the case. It hadn't even come close.

Yet Perles' statement was enough to satisfy most seg-
ments of society. That is sad. This book is not meant to
chastise the thousands of Americans who enjoy a good
football game. If there is an abundance of finger-pointing
in this book, then a certain share of the blame must come
back to the folks who have over-glorified these exploits
for far too long: members of the media. Successful teams
sell papers. Bowl-bound squads hike up the ratings. And,
while there surely is nothing wrong with secretly pulling
for a team to succeed because it makes good copy, it is
quite disturbing when beat reporters ignore ignoble behavior for the same reason. A sense of celebrity is rampant
among today's fraternity of highly paid college coaches.
Too many reporters spend their time sitting in the plush
offices of these mini-legends, chatting endlessly about the
upcoming battle, while vulnerable young athletes walk out
the door wondering how they will find the energy to study
for the next day's exam. But this matters little when the
man behind the desk—the man providing access—tells

reporters that academics come before football. *That* makes good copy.

To journalists schooled in cornering politicians and city officials, this lack of edge is glaringly apparent in most sportswriters. This isn't to say there aren't tough questions; there are. But they usually deal with mundane matters, such as Saturday's starting quarterback. Issues—real issues which examine the very structure of a coach's ethical principles—are largely nonexistent. As one Associated Press reporter, a veteran of Lansing's hard-news climate, remarked after attending a Perles press conference, "I could not get over how much sportswriters cowered around him. It was as if he were God. They just wrote down what he said, accepted it for truth, and said, 'Thank you, George.' I couldn't believe it."

It is a lethargy—a passive attitude of "Report the news, but don't make the coach angry"—that is prevalent in many newspapers. As a result, stories of issues that may inflict a change in the system are considered too risky to pursue.

What all this means is that we have to be a little less infatuated with the style of college football and more concerned with its substance. The game, of course, inspires us. It thrills us. There are few experiences richer than strolling next to the leaf-covered Red Cedar River on an autumn football Saturday. That should be the genuine joy of college athletics. Not the wins, not the Bowl appearances, and certainly not the twisted priorities. "I was at a Princeton–Columbia game last fall and it was such a joy to watch," says Professor Peter Levine. "There were about 8,000 fans gathered there, and it was more in keeping with a university setting and what college athletics should be. The kids looked like normal, average-size kids; they didn't look like they were on steroids. Though they took the game seriously, they weren't obsessed by it.

There wasn't that extreme pressure to perform. It wasn't a life-and-death situation."

Neither Michigan State nor any other major-college football program can ever return to that pristine soil again. It's naïve to think otherwise. The damage has been done.

"Everybody has lost their perspective on this: athletic departments, coaches and certainly the fans," says Beth Shapiro, who has studied Michigan State University's association with big-time sport. "It's a very complex problem and the solution is going to be a complex solution."

It is hoped that Perles, the athletic director, treats this dilemma with more thought than Perles, the head coach. His "family" deserves that much.

July 1990

THE AUTHORS

Stu Whitney and Bob Kourtakis, both graduates of Michigan State University with degrees in journalism, have written extensively about MSU football. Stu Whitney is a sportswriter for the Argos *Leader* in Sioux Falls, South Dakota. Bob Kourtakis is employed at Rossman Communications in Lansing, Michigan.

GV 958 .M5 W47 1990

Whitney, Stu, 1967-

Behind the green curtain

WITHDRAWN

STATE LIBRARY OF OHIO
SEO Regional Library
Caldwell, Ohio 43724

DEMCO